*Praise for*

# Bringing Out the Best in Others!

**"**I've practiced the three keys ever since I learned them from Tom in a seminar, and they have always boosted productivity. Every time!"

### Rick Erickson, CLU
**Managing Director**
**Principal Financial Group**
**Glendale, California**

**"**If you're connected with youth sports in any way, this book is a must read!"

### Fred C. Engh
**President & CEO**
**National Alliance for Youth Sports**
**West Palm Beach, Florida**

**"**This book is essential reading for every educator — from superintendents to parents! The three keys create an environment that helps each child achieve."

### Ashley Smith, Jr.
**Cleveland Middle School, Cleveland, Tennessee**
**Tennessee Middle School Principal of the Year**

**"**The success of any organization depends on the outstanding efforts of its people. *Bringing Out the Best* shares learning and lessons for leaders at every level to energize their teams."

### J. W. Marriott, Jr.
**Chairman and CEO**
**Marriott International**

"If you guide kids in any fashion — as a parent, coach, teacher, or mentor — read the book and put the three keys into practice. They're practical and they work."

**Greta Williams**
Executive Director
Big Brothers Big Sisters, A Community of Caring
Kalamazoo, Michigan

"These three keys are a battle plan for sustaining high performance from your team through any kind of economy."

**Gerald F. O'Connell**
CEO
Entuity, Inc.
New York City

"A must read for principals, teachers, and parents. Practicing the three keys brings about measurable results in just a short time. An invaluable tool!"

**Mark A. Kern**
New Palestine Elementary, New Palestine, Indiana
Indiana Elementary Principal of the Year

"Deceptively powerful. A straightforward and practical way to foster and develop peak performance in others. Read the book and put the three keys to work today."

**Jan Mulcrone**
Director, Human Resource Services
University of Michigan Health System
Ann Arbor, Michigan

**"**A commonsense approach to performance enhancement. Read it and increase your probability of coaching success."

**Jack H. Llewellyn, Ph.D.**
Sports Psychologist/Consultant, Atlanta Braves
Author, *Coming In First*

**"**If you want to grow your business, you need to read this book today and put the three keys to work."

**Rodger Ford**
Founder of AlphaGraphics
Tucson, Arizona

**"**From teachers to camp counselors, corporate trainers to hourly workers, *Bringing Out the Best in Others!* is a must read. All kids can achieve, given the right balance of the three keys."

**Susan L. Gutierrez**
Forest Hills Central Middle School, Grand Rapids, Mich.
Michigan Teacher of the Year

**"**An easy-to-read book that is chock full of practical advice for anyone in a leadership position. The three keys are particularly useful as a guide for performance improvement."

**Phyllis Freyer**
Senior Vice President
Lovelace Health Systems
Albuquerque, New Mexico

"Concrete information in an easy-to-read format. The quick lesson design is ideal. Read the book, use the keys, and watch productivity rise."

**Julie Scofield**
**Executive Director**
**Smaller Business Association of New England**

"Solid content. Well written. Practical. What more could you ask for in a book? Read it today."

**Randy Burns**
**Senior Vice President**
**Advest, Inc.**
**Hartford, Connecticut**

"This is an easy-to-read book that educators can use to directly and positively influence students' performance."

**David W. McKay**
**Aberdeen High School, Aberdeen, Washington**
**Washington Teacher of the Year**

"Anyone interested in motivating people should read this book. It's Tom Connellan at his best!"

**Ken Blanchard**
**Coauthor, *The One Minute Manager*® and *Whale Done!*™**

"If you're committed to kids in any way — as a parent, grandparent, coach, teacher, or mentor — you need to read this book and practice the three keys."

**Jack Canfield**
Coauthor, *Chicken Soup for the Soul®*

"It's amazing how this book brings concepts relating to business, parenting, and teaching all together in one medium that will help me be better at work, at home, and in life!"

**Leslie Beers**
Human Capital Associates, Inc.
Colorado Springs, Colorado

"A rare book. With skill and clarity, Tom teaches you three simple concepts that will change you and your organization for the better."

**Anthony J. DeFail, FACHE**
President/CEO
MMC Health Systems, Inc.
Meadville, Pennsylvania

"If you want to grow a successful business, this is a must-read book for you and the key members of your team."

**Dixon Doll**
Managing General Partner
DCM Doll Capital Management
Menlo Park, California

# Bringing Out the Best in Others!

*Three Keys for Business Leaders,*
*Educators, Coaches and Parents*

by

## Thomas K. Connellan, Ph.D.

**BARD PRESS**
Austin

# Bringing Out the Best in Others!

*Three Keys for Business Leaders, Educators, Coaches and Parents*

Bard Press
5275 McCormick Mtn. Dr.
Austin, Texas 78734
512-266-2112
www.bardpress.com

This is a work of fiction. All the characters and events portrayed herein are either fictitious or are used fictitiously.

**Ordering Information**

To order additional copies, contact your local bookstore or call 800-945-3132.

Quantity discounts are available.

ISBN 1-885167-58-X (hardcover)

**Library of Congress Cataloging-in-Publication Data**

Connellan, Thomas K., 1942-
    Bringing out the best in others! : 3 keys for business leaders, educators, coaches and parents / Thomas K. Connellan.
        p.    cm.
    Includes bibliographical references.
    ISBN 1-885167-58-X (cloth : alk paper)
    1. Employee motivation. 2. Expectation (Psychology) 3. Responsibility.
4. Feedback (Psychology) I. Title.
    HF5549.5.M63  C658 2002
    158.2--dc21

                                                         2002038574

**Credits**

    Developmental Editor: Jeff Morris
    Proofreading: Bobbie Jo Sims, Deborah Costenbader
    Cover design: Hespenheide Design
    Text design/illustration/production: Jeff Morris

First printing: January 2003

# Contents

# The Issues

## *Why Do Good People Fall Short?*

October 14, 8:30 A.M. In a small conference room, four men and two women were seated around a conference table. Tony Russo, the man at the head of the table, smiled at the others and spoke.

"Here's the drill," he said. "Each of you is here to tackle a problem you're having with someone you know who is underperforming. Today we'll get a handle on these problems and look at some proven techniques that will help you solve them. Along the way, I'll give you a framework for laying out your action plan to improve performance.

"Over the next ninety days, you'll put these techniques to work. Then we'll meet back here and swap stories to see how well you did. I've conducted hundreds of these programs, so I'm sure most of you — perhaps all of you — will have success stories to tell us. And some of you will find other ways you can use these tools besides addressing the specific problems you came here to solve. For now, though, we'll focus on what you came here for.

"Each of you has sent me a brief description of yourself and of the issue you're facing at work, at home, or in some other situation. I've also had a chat with each of you, in person or on the phone. So I know a little bit about you already. And I've provided each of you with a list of our ground rules — confidentiality, privacy, cell phones, and so forth — so I'll assume you're up to speed on those matters.

"Now, to get the ball rolling, I'd like you to tell me, and everyone else here, something about what you're up against. Describe your performance situation to the group. This can be a problem getting an employee or employees to perform well, achieving cooperation from fellow committee members, problems with your kids — any situation in which people don't do as you expect or want them to.

"Start by introducing yourself to the group, then describe where you work, what you do, who is involved, and so forth. Condense it into about a minute, and we'll go once around the room. Later we'll talk about our situations in more detail.

"Who's willing to go first? Good, let's start with you, Mary. Tell us what you do and the issue you want to resolve. You're a sales manager, right?"

Mary nodded. "Yes, I'm Mary Steena, and I'm the national sales manager for Caribou Creek. We distribute specialty food items through a variety of channels. I'm here because I'm having problems with a couple of my sales reps.

"Actually, I should qualify that. The problems I'm having with two of my salespeople — I'll just call them Marvin and Pat — are not unique. Every sales manager has trouble getting peak performance from all sales reps all the time. A certain amount of that is part of the psychology of sales. When it's hot, it's hot, and when it's not, it's not. People are more motivated when things are going well, and less motivated when items aren't selling.

"But Marvin is a special case, and that's why this bothers me so much. When he's on his game, there's nobody better at selling. But too much of the time he simply doesn't apply himself. Not only does it affect his own sales, but it affects overall sales, because the rest of the sales staff know how good a salesman he is, and they look up to him.

"I take him aside for a heart-to-heart talk, and he goes back out and beats his quota for a week or two. Then he lets things slide again. Another talk, and he's setting records again, but it never lasts.

"Pat is another story. He used to be good, almost as good as Marvin, but over the past year or two his performance has gone steadily downhill. Pat's got the skills and experience to be a top-notch sales rep, but he's just not performing. I talk with him and his performance improves, but not as much as it should. Then he slips —

kind of like Marvin, but a little lower than he was before. We talk again, and he improves again, then he slips again. So it's the same up-and-down as with Marvin, but with the slips frequently at a slightly lower level than before.

"I went to our VP of sales and marketing and told him I didn't know what else I could do to stop Pat's downhill slide, and that Marvin's ups and downs were affecting the whole sales staff. He sent me here."

"Thank you, Mary. Well stated. Now let me ask you something. What's your perception of where the problem lies? Is there something going on with Marvin and Pat that you don't know about or can't fix? Or do you think the problem comes from somewhere outside them — something to do with their interaction with the company?"

"I don't know, Tony. They never complain to me about anything, and when I talk with them about their performance, they don't blame anybody else — just the market, or the competition, or the pricing. If they're having trouble at home, I'm not aware of it."

"Okay," said Tony. "I know we can't answer this question up front, and the answer, whatever it might be, may only lead to part of the solution. I brought it up because it's important to ask questions even when we can't answer them. This is only one of the questions we need to keep in mind. And sometimes, part of the solution is to refer someone to Human Resources. Or with kids, it may be a clinical situation — they may need professional help.

"But I'll tell you this. We've had a lot of sales managers in this program, at least 200 over the past five years, and our results have been excellent — as you'll see.

"Let's hear next from the guy whose business is asking lots of questions — the teacher. Mike, why are you here?"

Mike, who was leaning back in his chair, sat forward quickly. "No fair, I didn't have my hand up." This got a laugh.

"Think of this as a pop quiz, Mike," replied Tony, bringing more laughs. "I think you explained in your letter that you were concerned about some of your brightest students."

"Yes, that's true. But I guess I'd have to say I'm concerned about all my students. Even though I teach fifth grade, I try to keep track of them down the line, and I see too many going out into the world not having discovered their full potential, not having the tools and skills and resources to realize it. As an educator, I think that's a terrible waste of a valuable resource. Oh, and my name's Mike Gwinn, and I teach here in Chatham.

"Mary told us about Marvin. Well, I sometimes feel like I have a whole classroom full of Marvins. A few of my kids are geniuses, a few are marginal achievers who try as hard as they can to keep up — but most are just average kids who don't seem to care much about the world outside their immediate circle of friends. They don't have any idea what they're capable of, what their untapped talents could mean to them and to the world.

"I went into teaching because I felt it was a good way to help make the world better. Even though I've become discouraged at how intractable this problem seems to be, I guess I'm still idealistic enough to want to make a difference. If I can come out of this program with just one good idea, I'll consider it time well spent."

> ❝ **If I can come out of this program with just one good idea, I'll consider it time well spent.** ❯❯

Tony said, "Yes, Mike, I think you'll gain more than one good idea during the time you spend here. And before this exercise ends, we'll all know what ideas you picked up and how useful they were in your situation because, as we work our way through, we're going to apply what we learn. I'll give you some tools to try out, along with some guidelines for applying them. Then, after you've had a chance to apply them, we'll meet once more to hear how well they've worked.

"It's unusual to have a teacher in a group of businesspeople, as you might have guessed, but it's not our first time. We've worked with educators before, and in most cases we've been able to raise test scores 5 to 10 percent on average. Not bad, eh?

"Now that we've heard Mike's concerns, let's take a look at a similar issue from the other side. I believe

Lloyd Magnusson is here strictly as a parent, and he's concerned that his daughter is not doing well in school. Is that right, Lloyd?"

Lloyd nodded. "Lori is a big worry for my wife and me. She does well on achievement tests, and she used to be among the top students in grade school. But now she seems to have lost interest in learning. She gets mostly C's and D's, with an occasional A or B. We can't seem to get her out of her slump. Sometimes we can't even get her to talk to us. When we do manage to get through to her, her grades usually go up, but before long they're down again."

"How old is she?"

"She's fourteen."

"I wonder," said Tony. "Have you thought this might be normal teenage rebellion? Or do you think it's something more?"

"I don't think that's quite it, although there's some of that going on. When she shuts herself off from us, it's more like she's disappointed in herself for not doing better. Sometimes she really applies herself, and she does seem pleased when she gets good results, like a B on a test or an essay. But then she loses interest, doesn't study, flunks a test, and gets even more discouraged. And her room gets even messier, which is another issue we're having with her."

"Well, Lloyd, I can't guarantee you can solve this problem overnight, but I can say this: your situation is not unique. We've dealt with this before and achieved some pretty good results. It's tough to see your own kid stumble, but you should know we've seen a lot worse and turned the situation around. So don't be discouraged.

"Yes, Janet?"

"Tony, I just want Lloyd to know that teenage girls are a mystery deeper than the ocean, and just about as scary. I know, because I was once a teenage girl and I've raised two of my own. And I did it the hard way, by instinct and guesswork — which in some cases means simply waiting it out. But from what I've heard about it, Lloyd, I think this program will help you understand and deal with it a lot faster than I was able to. And probably better."

"Thanks, Janet," said Tony. "And you're right. You'd be surprised at how many business managers have come up to me after one of these sessions and said, 'Tony, this is really good stuff, but I wish I'd known it when I was raising my kids!'

"**B**ut that's not what you're here for today, is it?"

"No, it's not," agreed Janet. "I'm Janet Patterson, and I'm here because I'm concerned about my grown-ups. I'm a nursing supervisor at Saint Joseph's Hospital. We're a community hospital, and I'm all too familiar with the pressures my people are under — life-and-death situations, bureaucratic foul-ups, too little money, too many patients, understaffing, the works. It can be stressful for all of us. And nurses who are under stress sometimes become poor team players. They stop helping and cooperating with one another. They don't pass along helpful information to the next shift. Their attitude becomes, 'My shift's over, it's been a bad day, I'm outta here.'

"These are good people. They're capable of doing wonderful things for their patients, even with the odds stacked against them. But when teamwork lags, that stacks the odds even more. I wish I knew how to get through to them — how to get them to put forth that little bit of extra effort that saves ten times as much work for someone else.

"I can get some of them to be good team players almost all of the time, and I can get all of them to be good team players some of the time. What I want is for all of them to be the best team players they can be, all of the time."

"Thank you, Janet. I think we'll soon discover ways to help you bring out the best in your nurses. You used the word 'teamwork,' and that's significant, because we've been very successful at improving teamwork in many different situations. And teamwork has a synergistic effect: small improvements in teamwork can create big improvements in overall results.

"Now, Carlos, that leaves you. Will you tell us your story?"

"Certainly," said Carlos. "I'm Carlos Navarro, and I'm the president of Arbor Paper Products here in Chatham. We produce pressure-sensitive products like mailing labels, product labels, and the stock postage stamps are made from. Chances are pretty good you use a lot of the products we manufacture.

"Our plant produces good results, but it's still not living up to its potential. Production volume is good, and product quality is good, but the plant has just never operated at its design potential.

"Even though our people believe they're giving it all they've got, I know there's another 2 to 3 percent productivity available to us, but it seems just out of reach. How do we tap that last bit of potential?

"These are good people. I can't push them any harder. I have to find ways of pulling them along. A colleague of mine told me this was the place to learn how to pull out that last 2 or 3 percent."

"Okay, thanks, Carlos. This program has been very successful in raising manufacturing productivity across a broad spectrum of industries. I can almost guarantee you'll achieve your efficiency goals. But I have to warn you — the bigger the company, the bigger the task.

"Folks, before we go on, does anybody have any questions? Comments?"

"Yes, Tony," said Mary. "At first I was a bit confused about why we seemed to be such a diverse group. I've known Carlos for some time, so his presence didn't surprise me. And I was talking with Janet before you came in and knew that she was a supervisor, like me. But when

I learned that Mike was a teacher and heard Lloyd mention something about his child, I wondered for a moment if this was going to be time well spent. I was concerned about what I perceived as 'nonbusiness' issues, like grades or parenting.

"But now I believe I understand what we have in common. Business is not the point. Although we are dealing with children and adults, with students as well as employees, what we share is performance issues — right? Getting someone to perform better or at least differently. It's all about human behavior. Each of us needs to get someone to behave differently — whether it's sales, quality, productivity, teamwork, grades, or something else."

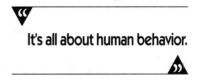

**It's all about human behavior.**

"That's a good insight, Mary. And it's the key to understanding the roadblocks you're all up against. There are more similarities than differences in your situations. For instance, take your sales reps, Marvin and Pat, and Lloyd's daughter, Lori. Each seems to improve after a heart-to-heart talk, but the improvement never lasts. That's a commonality, and both of you will walk away from here with a set of tools to resolve that up-down-up-down issue. You'll probably apply them differently, but the core skill will be the same.

"Same thing for everyone here. The tools that help Carlos get more out of his employees can help Mike get more out of his students. What works for Janet in dealing with teamwork at the hospital may be just the thing to help Carlos improve teamwork in his factory. Or, for that matter, in the youth soccer team he coaches.

"This is not an oversimplification of your issues, nor do I mean to imply that Marvin is a child, or that nurses work under the same conditions as salespeople. As you'll see, the tools we're talking about are universal. They work because they focus on changing behavior. If you apply them, they'll bring out the best in anyone — whether in business, school, community service, or the home. Some of your organizations may have mentoring programs, or perhaps you or someone you know is mentoring a student. The process and tools apply in these situations, too.

> **The tools we're talking about are universal. They work because they focus on changing behavior.**

"One more thing. As we move along, I'm going to ask each of you to get more specific about exactly what changes you'd like to see. We'll come to that later, but for now, just start thinking about it.

"In a few minutes I'll tell you what we've learned about the conditions that create high-performing individuals — what makes them tick. We'll discuss and analyze these conditions and how they can be created for the individuals you're concerned about.

"By the time we finish today, you'll have gained enough knowledge to go out and bring forth high performance from people you never thought capable of it. Consistently high performance, over the long term."

# Discovery

## *What Creates Consistently High Performance?*

Tony placed a small stack of papers on the table. He looked out at the five people seated around the table. "Let's see a show of hands. How many of you are 'only children'?"

Mary raised her hand.

"Now, all of you who are firstborns, raise your hands." Three more: Mike, Janet, and Lloyd. Mary hesitated, then lowered her hand. "You too, Mary. An only child counts as a firstborn. Carlos, what about you?"

"I was second youngest of six," said Carlos. "One older brother, four sisters."

"Interesting," said Tony. "Four out of five. In all the programs I've held on this topic, the average has been about 60 percent firstborns.

"You're wondering why I asked that, aren't you? It wasn't because I'm nosy. Although, as others will tell you, I am certainly a curious fellow." They chuckled.

"It's because of something I became aware of about ten years ago, when I first started looking at this whole issue of high performance. Whenever I talked with a manager, supervisor, team leader, or executive, I would ask questions about their top performers.

"A sales manager would say to me, 'What I need is four more reps like George.' Not having a clue about this George, I would ask for more details. 'Well, he's a top performer in every way,' the sales manager would say. 'He does his homework on what the customer needs. He goes into each call well prepared. He gets in the extra call at the end of the day. And it pays off — he's always number one or number two in everything we measure. Sales volume, gross margin dollars, new accounts, account retention, customer satisfaction — you name it, he's there.'"

"Can you give me George's phone number?" asked Mary. The others laughed. "I've got a spot for him. And his twelve brothers and sisters."

Tony smiled. "Nice try, Mary. Sorry, George is happily employed — or was, ten years ago. But you raise two interesting points. One is about the brothers and sisters. That's important, and I'll tell you why in a minute. The other point is that you probably already have several potential 'Georges' on your payroll. Marvin could be a 'George.' Maybe Pat, too. I'm going to show you how to tap into their full potential, and why you're going to see a bump in sales when you do. Ten percent, 20 percent, maybe even 30 percent. We've even gotten 40 to 50 percent improvement in a number of cases — and in a couple of instances involving just one individual and one product, we actually hit 200 percent. But 10 to 20 percent is the norm."

Tony could see, in their faces, the effect this information was having on the group. They were silently working the numbers, translating the "bump" into dollars, or perhaps grades — all except Lloyd, who asked, "What if we're not talking about sales or revenues? How do you translate that in terms of child rearing?"

"Good question, Lloyd. Of course we're talking about something much broader than just a company's bottom line. We're talking about the behaviors that bring such results. You'll see the same behavior improvements in Lori, Lloyd, although I doubt it will put your family in a higher tax bracket." Lloyd smiled.

"Now, in your case, Mike," continued Tony, "you'll see improvements you can measure in terms of your students' grades, attendance records, and so forth." Mike nodded. "And Janet will use other measures of improvement — staff going out of their way to help others, better working relationships with admitting or pharmacy — and if the studies I've read are right, that will lead to reduced treatment costs and potentially even shorter hospital stays.

"But whether you can measure them with actual numbers or not — and in most cases you can — you'll all see notable improvements after you've learned and applied the principles we're going to discuss here.

"To get back to my story: The sales manager was describing all the ways his top sales rep was great, but this didn't tell me *why* George was a cut above the others, *why* he was such a self-starter. It was the same with other people I talked to — department heads, engineering team leaders, principals, community leaders. Each would sing the praises of one or two outstanding performers.

"But I wasn't learning much about what caused the higher levels of performance. I was looking for a pattern, a system. I hoped to find something I could replicate and teach to others, but high achievers just seemed to happen.

"So I began to dig deeper. I asked questions about the high achievers' backgrounds. There were lots of possibilities — education, money, experience, the usual suspects. But these things didn't correlate with achievement as strongly as I had expected. Trying to find some factor that could reliably predict success was like searching for a diamond in a gravel pit.

"Then I discovered something odd. I read a report that said 64 percent of the people listed in *Who's Who* happened to be the oldest children in their families.

"One study doesn't mean much of anything in statistics, but it made me wonder: Could it actually be that simple? Could being a firstborn make such a difference?

"I began to check out the statistics on firstborns. And what I found amazed me. So if you're taking notes, here are a few facts to write down and think about.

"Fact number one: Two-thirds of all entrepreneurs are firstborns.

"Fact number two: Of the first twenty-three astronauts, twenty-one were firstborns.

"Fact number three: A ten-year study of 1,500 superior Wisconsin ninth-graders showed that 49 percent of them were firstborns."

"That's a nice set of facts," said Carlos. "But what's the relevance? We're here to brush up on our leadership skills, not to learn how to recruit firstborns, right?"

"Of course," replied Tony. "The same thought occurred to me. But you're just a little ahead of the story. Stay with me a minute and you'll see the point.

"More facts: Female world leaders between 1960 and 1999 — 45 percent were firstborn.

"Firstborns are twice as likely to become CEOs as laterborns.

"Fifty-five percent of all supreme court justices have been firstborns.

"Over half of United States presidents have been firstborns.

"Here's an interesting finding. One study showed that more than half the people elected president of the American Psychological Association were firstborns. Incidentally, it's the same with people who were elected to the National Academy of Sciences. And according to a study done in 1874, firstborns were overrepresented among fellows of the Royal Society, England's distinguished scientific academy."

> **Over half of United States presidents have been firstborns.**

"When you say 'overrepresented,' what percentage would you expect?" asked Mike. "Maybe there are just more firstborns than people realize."

"Good question, Mike. In the general population, firstborns make up about 35 percent — including, as I said, 'only' children. This gives us a basis for comparison. For example, in one air force study, about 80 percent of high-achieving military pilots were firstborn. That's more than twice the percentage you'd expect if being firstborn made no difference.

"Here's more: 55 percent of highly creative scientists at one major chemical company — 'creative' meaning having a Ph.D. and getting more than one patent a year — were firstborns."

Carlos leaned forward in his chair. "Just out of curiosity, do you ever find any firstborns among the lowest performers?"

"As a matter of fact, yes. For example, in the last study I mentioned, the chemical company, 14 percent of the 'low creative' scientists — that is, Ph.D.s with zero patents per year — were firstborns. In other words, being firstborn is not a guarantor of success — just a strong indicator.

"Now, this brings us to the issue Carlos brought up a minute ago: the leadership issue.

"This is a leadership program, not an employment practices seminar. We're not here to learn how to round up firstborns and pen them in our corral. That's labor intensive, not worth the effort you'd have to spend to do it, and it's no guarantee of success. And — although I'm no lawyer — it's probably illegal.

"But Carlos's question leads to another, more interesting set of questions: What is it about firstborns that makes them top performers? Can we identify the environmental factors that tend to lead to higher levels of performance among firstborns? And can we use these factors to make a top performer — or at least a significantly better performer — out of any associate or employee? Or any committee member? Or any team or task force member? Or any student? Or any child?

"Starting with the people we have, how do we bring out the best in them? How do we tap their full potential? Not everyone can be great, but most can be better than they are. By leadership alone, can we get others to perform at higher levels simply by tapping into their full potential?

> ❝
> **Not everyone can be great, but most can be better than they are.**
> ❯❯

"You'll notice that I'm limiting this discussion to environmental factors, not genetic ones."

"Yes," said Carlos with a grin. "As fifth out of six, I was ready to challenge if you brought up genetics."

Tony and the others laughed. "Good. You'll be happy to know that the only mention I'm going to make is this: There is no scientific evidence, or even basis, for the idea that the order of birth affects genetic makeup.

"But let me cut to the chase. I went looking for environmental factors. Specifically, what was different about the way firstborns were raised? About the way they were treated by the people around them, their parents, their schools? There are lots of possibilities, of course. Things like being raised by younger parents, which as we all know has its downside as well as its advantages.

"I read the psychology journals. I talked with child psychologists. I interviewed parents. I watched families in action. I learned a lot, and I identified dozens, maybe hundreds of things that could potentially influence success in life.

"But when it came to the differences between firstborns and the rest of the children in a family, there were three factors that stood above the rest. Firstborns get more positive expectations, more responsibility, and more feedback.

"These are worth writing down and thinking about. In fact, we'll be talking about them for the rest of the day.

"First factor." Tony turned and scrawled a large number "1" on the chalkboard behind him, followed by a single word:

## 1. EXPECTATIONS

"Expectations. People have more positive expectations for firstborns. They're going to be president of the senior class, the all-star quarterback, head cheerleader, captain of the tennis team. Whatever they're involved in, they're expected to excel.

## 2. RESPONSIBILITY

"Second factor: Firstborns are given more responsibility, and at an earlier age. They're asked to look after and help take care of their younger brothers and sisters. When they all go to the movies together, or to the mall, or out to the street to meet the ice cream truck, the oldest is given the money, the cell phone, the directions on how to get there, what to buy, what not to do.

## 3. FEEDBACK

"Third factor: Firstborns get more feedback. They get more attention from parents, relatives, family friends. They have more pictures taken. Parents spend more time encouraging them to walk and talk.

"To me, this was very exciting information. It meant that we could actually identify three distinct conditions that tend to make firstborns better-than-average achievers. And having identified them, we could examine them, and study them, and learn from them. Then, perhaps, we could replicate them in other situations —

business offices, retail stores, classrooms, civic organizations, even sports.

"You see, the important thing to keep in mind is that these factors are not intrinsic to firstborns. They are plainly environmental. And here's the most wonderful, amazing thing about them: it's the *presence* of the three factors that makes the difference. It's not about being firstborn — it's about the presence of the three factors. Sure, they happen to be present more often with firstborns than with those born later. But when we've put these three factors into practice with later-born children, they have worked there as well. When we used the factors on a sales team, they worked there. When we applied them to manufacturing, they worked again. In short, everywhere we've tried them, they've worked.

> **❝** Expectations, responsibility, feedback — it's the *presence* of these factors that makes the difference. **❯❯**

"I discovered this when I dug deeper beneath the surface of what makes top performers. The more research I did, the more top performers I found who didn't necessarily match the 'first child' pattern.

"For example, I talked with a number of high-performing and low-performing sales reps in wholesale distribution companies. Mary, I know this will interest you. In one study, I found quite the reverse of what I expected — there were more firstborns among the low performers than among the high performers.

"I thought, What the heck is going on here?

"But I kept talking with people. I began to focus more on the leaders, and I discovered something very interesting. The leaders of the high performers were actually creating the three factors in the job setting. That is, they were supplying the environment that usually gives the firstborn an advantage.

"In another of my sales rep studies, I focused specifically on how good the sales managers were at introducing the three factors into the workplace, and I designed a test to measure the results. And sure enough, the managers of the high performers scored 22 percent higher in their ability to create the three factors than the managers of the low performers.

"I interviewed company presidents who achieved that position before age forty. I didn't find as many firstborns as I expected, but I discovered something just as significant. Two-thirds of them could identify a supervisor or manager or mentor from earlier in their career who created the factors in the job climate.

"The effects of expectations, responsibility, and feedback are age independent. They are something you can put into the work environment to improve the performance of adults. Janet, you can build them into your interactions with your nursing team, the administration, the pathology lab, and other departments to improve communication, attention to detail, cooperation — in other words, teamwork. Mary, you can apply them to your problems with Marvin and Pat to make them full-time top performers — and, not incidentally, raise the performance level of the whole sales staff. Carlos, you'll find it will help you raise throughput, product quality, and most other measures of productivity.

"And, of course, Mike and Lloyd can use them on their kids, who are still in their formative years." The two men nodded hesitantly.

Tony sat without speaking for a few moments. He studied the faces around the table. Janet was still hurriedly scribbling notes. Mary was tapping her teeth with the eraser end of her pencil. Carlos sat back with his fingers interlaced, lost in his own thoughts.

"Okay, right now you've probably got a lot going on in your heads. You may be thinking, 'Interesting, but how do I put it to work?' Or 'I think I'm doing some of this now.' Or maybe 'Hmm — I'm doing pretty good on two of the factors, but not so good on the third.' What I usually find is that people are already using some of these factors but haven't put them together in a coordinated way. It's almost certain that you've used them in situations where you've succeeded.

"Let me ask you a question. What have you done for yourself lately? Think of some personal goal you've set for yourself, one that you've followed through on and accomplished. Like learning a new computer program or losing weight or mastering Thai cooking."

Lloyd's eyes lit up in recognition.

"Yes, Lloyd?"

"A few years ago I decided I needed to lose a lot of weight and get in shape. So I set up a training schedule for myself. You know, daily and weekly goals for running, weight training, calorie intake, and so forth. I charted my progress, kept at it for many months, and finally reached my weight and strength goals."

"So you began the program in the expectation that you would achieve your goals, didn't you?"

"Yes, of course," said Lloyd. "Otherwise, I suppose, I wouldn't have bothered to start."

"You gave yourself the first essential condition: positive expectations. The fact that you expected to accomplish your goals made reaching them almost inevitable, didn't it? I like to repeat what Henry Ford said: 'Whether you think you can or whether you think you can't, you're right.' As a leader, your job is to help them think they can."

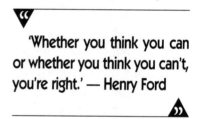

'Whether you think you can or whether you think you can't, you're right.' — Henry Ford

"That's a good quote," said Mike. "I think I'll frame that and hang it in my classroom."

"Think about the second factor," Tony went on. "Responsibility. How did you take responsibility for achieving your goal?"

Lloyd thought for a moment. "By posting my goals on my kitchen wall. I couldn't miss seeing them every day, and to keep my conscience from bothering me, I stuck to the schedule. Is that what you mean?"

"Exactly," said Tony. "You took the responsibility for your own actions. You set up meaningful but realistic targets, using short-range and long-range goals you felt you could achieve. You didn't leave yourself any room to make excuses, such as deciding your goals were too ambitious or that you didn't have enough time to spend on them. You planned responsibly, and you followed through on the plan responsibly.

"The third factor, feedback, is one you also built into your plan. You posted your goals for yourself, then you recorded your progress, day by day and week by week. In doing so, you encouraged yourself to keep working toward subsequent goals."

"Yes, you're right. I started walking and running six miles a week and got up to running four miles, four times a week — which I still do regularly. Took me six months to get there."

"Good for you. Congratulations! So in meeting your goals and recording your progress at regular intervals, you achieved a feeling of accomplishment, which made it easier to stay on the program and reach the next milestone. That's feedback. And it's the third of the three factors that you've created for yourself.

"**N**ow, this is what you're going to learn to do for your folks at work, your students, your children. In this program, you will learn the principles in much more detail. You will devise ways to apply these principles to your individual situations. You will set goals to accomplish in order to address your issues. And you will measure the progress in a feedback loop of your own devising.

"You will learn how to introduce all three factors into your leadership practices, your relationships with the people you lead. You will find that these people will respond positively to the presence of these factors just the way others have responded — by boosting their performance.

"You will achieve results you didn't think possible. Your low achievers will become high achievers. Your apathetic people will become engaged and more productive.

"The difference is that all of you, I can say with some assurance, are already self-starters. You're accustomed to creating these conditions for yourself, and that's why you're successful at reaching most of the goals you set for yourself. You enjoy the process of setting goals and achieving them.

"Each of you has described the person or persons whose performance you're concerned about. Now you will learn how to give them

> **Believe in 'em, hold 'em accountable, and give 'em supportive feedback.**

the same joy of accomplishment. That's why you're here.

"Over the next several hours, you're going to hear three messages about bringing out the best in others — believe in 'em, hold 'em accountable, and give 'em supportive feedback. You'll learn how the three factors work, the tools you can use to apply them, and the structures for putting them into practice. That's what we'll hold *you* accountable for.

"Then I'm going to turn you loose for ninety days. At the end of that time, we'll meet again. You'll tell me, and your fellow participants, what you've done and how well it worked, and we'll discuss your actions and the results. In other words — feedback.

> **You will succeed. You'll even surprise yourselves.**

"And I have the highest expectations of all of you." He smiled. He could feel the excitement building in the room.

"You will succeed. You'll even surprise yourselves."

# Expectations

## *The Power of the Positive*

After the break, Tony came back into the room carrying two thick textbooks. He dropped the books heavily on the table and shook his arm, as though to get the circulation going again. He looked up at his group, who were filing back into the room, and smiled slyly.

"Ancient Greek mythology," he whispered.

This was greeted with silence, except for a muffled groan from Mary.

"Well, maybe just a brief refresher course. Can you take about five minutes of Greek mythology, Mary?"

Mary laughed. "Sure. I was just thinking about a semester in high school a long time ago. Never could keep those characters straight."

"Well, the character I want to talk about is someone most of you have probably heard of. How many of

you have seen the musical *My Fair Lady*? Or the movie?"
All except Carlos raised their hands.

"Do you know what that musical was based on?"
asked Tony.

"Wasn't it *Pygmalion*, by George Bernard Shaw?"
said Mike.

"Spoken like a true schoolteacher," said Tony. "Mike
is correct. It was based on Shaw's play, which was in turn
based on the Greek myth of Pygmalion." Tony opened
one of the books to a paper-clipped page and held it up
for everyone to see.

"Pygmalion was a sculptor who created a statue of
the ideal woman, then fell in love with his own creation,
even believing her to be a real person. Aphrodite, the
goddess of love — the Romans called her Venus — took
pity on him and brought his statue to life.

"Centuries later, Shaw retold *Pygmalion* as the story
of Professor Henry Higgins and Eliza Doolittle, an illit-
erate Cockney flower girl. In Shaw's version, Higgins, a
professor of linguistics, makes a bet with a colleague that
he can pass Eliza off as a duchess by changing the way
she speaks. Thanks to his expectations — and a lot of
hard work — he is able to do so.

"Yes, Carlos? You seem a bit skeptical."

Carlos, who had been leaning back in his chair with
his arms crossed, said, "Well, I'm not sure where you're
going, but if you're saying all it takes is high expectations, I have a problem with this. I have high expectations
that my company's product quality can be made better,
and I speak to my managers about this constantly, but

it doesn't seem to be happening. At least not the way you seem to be saying."

"Well, Carlos, let's look at that. I noticed that you're using the term 'high expectations.' I prefer 'positive expectations.' Here's why. You can have high expectations — that is, expect a lot from people — but at the same time you may not believe they can actually succeed. 'Positive expectations' means believing they can succeed. And you have to believe that in order to make it happen.

"Of course, positive expectations by themselves are not enough. They're only one of three ingredients for bringing out the best in others. And even then, positive expectations are not effective in a vacuum. They have to be communicated to others, and understood, and accepted.

"It may be that you need to take it further. Remember, you're only one of many people interacting with those who affect productivity. You have positive expectations, but perhaps there are a hundred people with negative expectations between you and them. If that's the case, your major task will be to see that your expectations get communicated to those in the middle, and accepted, and understood — and passed on.

"There's an interesting study in my files that's right down your alley, Carlos. Do you know what year the U.S. Census Bureau began to automate its census tabulation?"

"No, I don't. Around 1960, I would guess."

"Nope. It was 1890. A mechanical engineer named Herman Hollerith invented a machine that could be used to enter census data on punch cards. The machine was something like a typewriter, and operators had to be specially trained. Hollerith estimated that a skilled operator might be able to process 550 cards per day. Sure enough, when workers were trained, they punched 550 cards per day with two weeks' experience. Some managed 700, but they complained that it was a real strain to work that fast.

"Well, the next group of operators were trained by people who had no knowledge of Hollerith's prediction. These operators weren't told anything about the first group. Before long, they were punching out 2,100 cards a day without breaking a sweat.

"This is a case in which artificially low expectations were communicated to one group of trainees but not to another. The machines didn't change, the training methodology didn't change, the trainees were no smarter or more adept than the early trainees. The only thing that changed was expectations.

"You may find that something like this is happening in your company, Carlos. You may be communicating positive expectations, but someone else may not. Or maybe you expect a lot but don't have positive expectations for people. Or maybe the positive expectations are there but are just not being communicated in a way that people experience as positive. But for now, let's just deal with the Pygmalion effect as a person-to-person thing. Okay?"

"Okay by me," replied Carlos. "That's a rather amazing story, if it's true."

"Oh, it's well documented, believe me. And it's only one of several hundred studies that show the impact of the Pygmalion effect in everyday life. Some of these studies are in educational settings, others in work settings. The conclusions are the same in all cases. Every one of us can significantly affect others simply by having positive expectations for them."

"Excuse me, Tony," said Janet. "Is this anything like the placebo effect?"

"Yes, it's related. Is anybody here unfamiliar with the placebo effect?"

"Refresh my memory," said Lloyd.

"Let's hear it from an expert in the field. Janet?"

"It's a well-established phenomenon in medicine," Janet explained. "A long time back, before there were many effective medicines available, or when a specific medical reason for an ailment could not be identified, doctors used to give patients 'medicine' containing nothing but sugar and tell them it would make them feel better. Even though there was no real medicine in them, the pills worked. Patients got better because they expected to get better.

"These sugar pills were called 'placebos.' These days, placebos are used in clinical studies to determine how effective new medications are. If you give patients anything at all, you heighten their expectations of getting well. So if 500 people take the medicine being tested for effectiveness and 500 get a placebo, and the same percentage get well, you can conclude that the new medicine is no more effective than simple positive expectations."

"But from what Tony told us," said Mary, "wouldn't the Pygmalion effect depend on the expectations of the doctor doing the prescribing? The doctor knows the placebo is basically worthless, so wouldn't his low expectations influence the outcome?"

"Yes," said Janet. "That's why most clinical trials today are double blind. That is, neither the physician nor the patient knows who's getting the placebo and who's getting the real thing until the study is over. That way, any differences between test groups can be related entirely to which dosage they received. It's still true that simply being in the study can boost a patient's expectations, but that effect is the same for both groups."

"Just how powerful is the placebo effect, Janet?" asked Lloyd.

"It depends on which study you look at. Some studies show an impact as high as 50 percent — meaning that half of the improvement is attributable to the placebo. A couple of studies seem to show 70 or 80 percent. Still others show hardly any effect at all. But the average is around 30 percent."

"Is this for serious illness, or just things like colds and flu?"

"It's interesting you should mention colds and flu, Lloyd. A lot of antibiotics are prescribed for colds and flu, even though viruses aren't affected by antibiotics. But people believe antibiotics will help, so in some cases they do help.

"As for other illnesses, a lot of conditions respond to placebos — hypertension, asthma, depression — oh my gosh, I just remembered something! This is almost unbelievable, but there was one study where they were testing how well a surgical procedure worked in treating angina pectoris. That's a chronic pain in the chest caused by a narrowing of the coronary arteries. The surgery involves closing off another artery in the chest. Anyway, they used a surgical placebo for the study — that is, they anesthetized some patients and just cut the skin. Here's what's amazing: 80 percent of the placebo patients, the ones who didn't get the actual surgery, got better, but only 40 percent of those who got the surgery improved. The placebo was actually better than the treatment!"

Tony interrupted: "Janet, do you know of any negative placebos? That is, cases where expectations made an illness worse?"

"Yes, there was a case in which one group of people were given sugar water but told it was an emetic — something that makes you vomit. Know how many of them vomited? Eighty percent. They call that a 'nocebo,' by the way."

"That is interesting," said Tony. "The reason I asked is because I was thinking of the Hollerith card-punch machine again. When people were told they probably wouldn't be able to turn out much more than 550 cards a day, they actually felt tired and overworked doing 700, although others easily punched three times as many. That's just like a negative placebo.

"Now, let's pull this together. To sum up what Janet has told us, a placebo can work positively or negatively, pretty much according to expectations. If the patient believes it will help, it will. And just as important, if the doctor believes it will help the patient, it probably will, because the patient's expectations are influenced by the doctor's."

"So what you're saying," said Mary, "is that the same thing happens in our everyday interactions with others. Kind of a placebo effect."

"Yes, exactly. In fact, here's a question for all of you. Can you give me an example from your own experience when your expectations may have influenced the actions or success of others?"

There was a moment of silence as they searched their memories. Then Mike said, "I'll have to confess, I had a student a few years ago who came dragging into his first class looking like a real sad sack — you know, beat-up clothes, bad haircut, slumped down in his chair. Thinking back on this, I'm sure I assumed he had an attitude, so I didn't pay much attention to him. But in the very first week he aced a test and volunteered for an extra-credit assignment. He turned out to be an intelligent, highly motivated student who just didn't look the part. My expectations for him were pretty low, so at first I probably paid more attention to students who I thought seemed eager to learn. Fortunately, he didn't let my expectations drag him down. He was unusual — self-motivating."

"That's a great example, Mike. Now let me give you some other cases that illustrate the effect expectations can have. Dr. Albert S. King — a Ph.D.-type doctor — worked with a group of fifty-six underprivileged, unskilled, or unemployed laborers who were being given specialized training in mechanical skills. He randomly selected fourteen of them and designated them 'high aptitude personnel' — HAPs, for short. Their supervisors were told to expect unusual improvement in the skills of these elite fourteen during training.

"Interesting things began to happen. While undergoing training, all the welders and mechanics were given practical and written tests, and those labeled 'high aptitude' scored higher than the others. All trainees were asked to rate their colleagues. Who would they most like to work with? Be with? Who were the best performers overall? Again, the HAPs got the highest scores.

"At the end of the program, the supervisors were asked to rate each trainee's development according to eight criteria. These were the results: the 'high aptitude personnel' scored much higher than the rest. They were judged more knowledgeable about their jobs, more productive, better able to learn their duties, more responsible, more cooperative, more logical.

According to their supervisors, the HAPs were the best performers.

"In reality, the only difference between the fourteen 'high aptitude' trainees and the others was in the minds of the supervisors. At least, this was true in the beginning, because they were chosen entirely at random.

"Obviously, positive expectations were at work here. How did the supervisors reveal their expectations to the selected trainees? Probably unconsciously, and in ways so subtle that trainees were not consciously aware of them.

"King devised a test for one possible visual cue. A sample of trainees from both groups were shown two photographs of the same supervisor. The photos were identical, except that one had been modified to make the supervisor's pupils appear larger. The trainees were asked two questions: (1) 'Do you see any differences in these pictures of your supervisor?' (2) 'Whether you see any differences or not, can you select the photo that shows how the supervisor usually looks at you?'

> ❝
> **Without being aware of it, we often tell others what we expect of them simply by the way we make eye contact.**
> ❯❯

"None of the trainees could identify any differences between the photos. However, all five 'high aptitude' trainees who were tested chose the large-pupil photo as the way their supervisors usually looked at them; only two out of seven undesignated trainees chose the modified photo.

"Why did the HAP trainees select the large-pupil photo, even when they couldn't put their finger on the difference? According to other psychological research, large pupil size can indicate more favorable attitudes and expectations. King concluded that one way the supervisors unintentionally communicated positive expectations was by eye contact.

"Without being aware of it, we often tell others what we expect of them simply by the way we make eye contact. And even though they may not realize what's happening, they feel the impact of our expectations. Even the non-HAP trainees in King's study probably got the message, perhaps through the supervisors' unconscious visual cues, that others among them were 'destined' for higher achievement.

"What does this mean for you?" asked Tony, making eye contact with each of his students in turn. "It means that to bring out the best in your employees — or your students or children — every fiber in your body, every cell in your being must communicate positive expectations. All your messages, spoken and unspoken, conscious and unconscious, must be congruent. If they're in conflict, the receiver will select one channel or the other to believe. We know from other research that if there's a conflict, for example, between your spoken words and

> **All your messages, spoken and unspoken, conscious and unconscious, must be congruent.**

your nonverbal cues, the nonverbal cues have a greater impact than the words. Mike, you gave us a perfect example of this — your high achiever whose body language gave you the wrong message.

"In my work with individuals like you, I often see parents, leaders, people in committee meetings saying one thing with their words but something different with their body language. You can say to your child, 'I'm ready to listen to your explanation,' but if you're standing there with your arms folded, glaring down at him, your body language is saying, 'My mind is already made up, and you're in trouble.' I see you nodding, Lloyd. Does this sound familiar?"

"Yeah, I'm afraid so. It's so easy to get into that pattern with kids, you know. I guess it's because they haven't learned to mask their body language. They squirm, they stick out their lower lip, they roll their eyes. Pretty soon, even though you don't want to, you find yourself speaking the same language."

"Amen!" said Janet.


"You know, Tony, that's something I've learned in teaching," said Mike. "Children are very impressionable, especially young children. They pick up on your mood without your having to say anything. If you don't have your mind right when you walk into the classroom, you can expect to have a tough day teaching. Do you have any studies that talk about the classroom?"

"As a matter of fact, I do," said Tony. "Robert Rosenthal and Lenore Jacobson got results similar to Al King's in a West Coast school system. After testing the IQs of students very carefully to establish a baseline, they selected several students at random in each classroom to be designated 'bright learners.' They told the teachers that these individuals had been identified by a psychological testing service as students who would learn a lot during the school year.

"At the end of the semester, the students were tested again. Not only did the students get better grades and better personality ratings from the teachers, they showed a significant rise in IQ scores."

"I'm sure that's true," said Mike. "I've seen poor students suddenly start doing better just because somebody said hello to them in the hall. I get the feeling that some of these kids don't get any attention at all."

"The same influences work in sales, Mary," said Tony. "J. Sterling Livingston studied a district sales manager who basically reorganized his entire sales crew. He assigned his best agents to work with his best assistant manager, the next-best agents with an average boss, and the low producers with the person he considered his least able supervisor. Here's what happened.

"Grouping the best salespeople with the top assistant manager increased their sales. They were nicknamed the 'Super Staff.' Their esprit de corps was very high, and they did even better than the district manager expected.

"The low producers, working with the least able assistant manager, sold even less than they had before.

Not only that, but more of them quit their jobs. So far, not too surprising, right?

"It was the middle group that had the most interesting result. The district manager expected only average performance from the group, and figured the salespeople would perform about the same as before. Instead, their sales improved markedly. Their assistant manager refused to believe he was any less capable than the leader of the Super Staff or that his people were less able than the salespeople in the top group. He continually communicated his positive expectations to his group, telling them that through persistence and hard work they could perform just as well. The middle group increased its production by a higher percentage than the Super Staff.

"I've found at least a hundred studies that say pretty much the same thing. And the thing they are all saying is that *your* expectations have a significant impact on the performance of others. Mary, your expectations are a big factor in getting results out of your Marvins. And Lloyd, the same holds true with your daughter; Carlos, with your entire production staff; Janet, with your nursing staff; Mike, with your students.

> Your expectations have a significant impact on the performance of others.

"If you expect the best from people, and if you communicate it clearly and consistently through your words, your tone of voice, your body language, and your communication setting, people will respond.

"Understand that I'm not equating positive expectations with positive thinking. Positive thinking often has nothing to do with reality. Unless positive thinking is translated into specific behavioral patterns, there's no impact.

**Positive expectations, as we define them here, must begin from current reality.**

"Positive expectations, as we define them here, must begin from current reality. If sales are down, that's a fact. If quality is poor, that's also a fact. You have to recognize the facts and accept reality. Looking at current reality usually requires a brutal assessment of where you really are. Until you've acknowledged things as they are, it's virtually impossible to move ahead. However, once you've accepted current reality, you can put positive expectations to work and change that reality to a different reality — a reality where productivity is improved, grades are higher, and teamwork is better."

# Accountability

## *The Strength of Discipline*

"Okay, let's look at the second factor — accountability," said Tony. "Here's a question for all of you: What's the number-one requirement for getting things done?"

There was an uneasy silence, as if he had uttered the fearsome words "pop quiz."

"I would say the will to do it," Mary offered.

"Yes, in a way. Anyone else?"

"Plans and objectives," said Carlos.

"That's two things, but they're not quite what I'm getting at. Anyone else?"

Silence.

"The answer I'm looking for is this: Someone's got to do it."

Carlos shook his head and smiled. "Too easy, Tony."

"Yes," said Tony. "Too easy. Too obvious. That's why everybody misses it. It's such an important factor that we tend to overlook it.

"Have you ever seen individuals or teams start out with the best of intentions but never accomplish a thing?"

Several of the group murmured, "Yes."

"When you see that going on, accountability is usually a key issue. Without accountability, nothing ever really gets done. Too often what you hear is 'That's everybody's responsibility.' But when profits, sales, quality, or customer relations is at stake, that's nonsense. Someone, some identifiable person, has to 'own' the goal. Although many may play a role in getting to the final result, someone has to be ultimately accountable. Anything that is 'everyone's responsibility' quickly becomes no one's responsibility. Lack of accountability simply paves the way to mediocrity.

> "
> **Lack of accountability simply paves the way to mediocrity.**
> ＂

"This is particularly true in individual efforts. Too many people wait around for something to happen, hoping for the best. They seem to be waiting for someone else to take the lead — even if the task at hand is something they are uniquely suited to do.

"One of my favorite phrases is 'No one is coming.' This is another way of saying, 'No use waiting for someone else to start things rolling. It's up to you.'

"What are the key ingredients in making accountability work for you?" Tony erased the chalkboard and scrawled:

### 1. ESTABLISH ACCOUNTABILITY

"The first is to assign accountability — but without assigning blame. Accountability is positive. Blame is negative. Doesn't get you anywhere." Beside the first entry he wrote "BLAME" on the chalkboard and drew a big circle and crossbar over it:

### 1. ESTABLISH ACCOUNTABILITY

"Second, you need clear-cut goals.

### 2. SET GOALS

"Be sure everyone involved understands the goal. Doesn't do much good to start off down the road if you haven't agreed on where you need to end up. No surprise there — right, Carlos?" Carlos smiled and nodded.

## 3. DEVELOP ACTION PLANS

"Third, you need an action plan for how the goal is going to be reached. Goals aren't reached by accident; they are achieved by design. Think of an action plan as an insurance policy that the goal will be reached.

## 4. ENGAGE

"The fourth ingredient is engagement. The more that people are engaged in identifying goals, developing plans, and measuring progress, the more accountable they become."

"Excuse me, Tony," said Lloyd. "I don't mean to throw cold water on the discussion, but this sounds like something business types do in long meetings with lots of people sitting around a table. Isn't it a bit much to expect a father and daughter to follow all these procedures? Positive expectations I can see, but no teenager's going to want to sit through a planning and goal-setting meeting."

"I understand, Lloyd," replied Tony. "But as you'll see, it sounds more complicated than it really is. Especially for a simple one-on-one, the kind you need. Stay with me on this.

"Let's go ahead and get into the first point, and I think you'll begin to see what I mean." Tony walked to the chalkboard and circled the word "ACCOUNTABILITY."

"As I said before, accountability is good, blame is bad. How do you make people accountable without playing the blame game?

"Two organizations that I see doing a great job of this are the United States Army and GE. Truth of the matter is that *all* the services do a great job — each in its own way. It's just that I have more direct experience with the army. Anyway, the army and GE make a practice of dealing with the facts of a situation without getting into the kind of pass-the-buck politics that can become a quagmire. The army begins creating this culture during basic training. It *sounds* tough; it *looks* tough; it *is* tough. But done properly, it teaches the recruit the importance of accountability.

"Some of you may remember the drill. It goes something like this:

"'Russo, did you knock over the box of MREs?' That's meals ready to eat, for you civilian types." A chuckle went around the table.

"'Sir, I did not knock over the MREs!'

"'Who DID knock them over, Russo?'

"'Smith did, sir!'

"'Russo, why didn't you stop Smith?'

"'I don't know, sir.'

"'I CAN'T HEAR YOU, RUSSO!!!'

"'I DON'T KNOW, SIR!!!'

"'YOU DON'T KNOW *WHAT*, RUSSO?'

"'*SIR, I DON'T KNOW WHY I DIDN'T STOP SMITH, SIR!!!*'

"'Well, Russo, do you think the next time you see that Smith is about to knock over the box of MREs *YOU MIGHT JUST BE ABLE TO STOP HIM?!?*'

"'*SIR, THE NEXT TIME SMITH IS ABOUT TO KNOCK OVER THE MREs, I WILL BE ABLE TO STOP HIM, SIR!*'"

Everybody around the table was grinning now, except Mike, who seemed momentarily lost in his own memories. Tony continued:

"The new recruit learns two things from exchanges like this — as does everybody else in the platoon. Russo learns to take responsibility for both his actions and his failure to act. So does Smith. By the time most people reach adulthood, they've picked up certain habits, such as avoiding responsibility and not facing facts. That's why the army — and other military services — are so tough during basic training. It takes strong discipline to break those bad habits.

"The army reinforces this retraining by conducting AARs — that's 'after action reviews.' These occur after every identifiable event, no matter how big or small, and they take maybe ten or fifteen minutes. Each review asks four simple questions: (1) What was supposed to happen? (2) What actually happened? (3) What accounts for any difference? (4) What can be learned? There are no memos. Nothing goes in anyone's personnel file. No one is put on report. The reviews are simple and straight-forward. They're not blaming sessions — they're learning opportunities, and although I was uncomfortable at first accepting responsibility, I soon saw them as an opportunity to learn and grow.

"I had an army Ranger instructor in a session here maybe ten months ago, and he told me they still use this approach. He also e-mailed me about three or four months later and said that adding positive expectations and increasing positive feedback was helping him improve the performance of his trainees.

"Jack Welch did the same thing at GE. He turned meetings into — as he described them — 'interactive forums for disseminating new ideas and sharing experiences.' He found this to be an effective weapon against workplace politics. These meetings brought facts to the surface and solved problems quickly. Despite its huge size, GE developed the response time of a much smaller company. Welch's innovations are one of the reasons GE grew into such a formidable competitor in the '80s and '90s.

"Nothing too complicated about any of this, is there? It's simple steps, like asking these four AAR questions, that can help establish accountability and get things done. If you're a sales rep, you can ask yourself these questions after every call. Carlos, you can ask your manufacturing teams. Lloyd, you can talk about these questions with your daughter.

"Each situation has to be handled differently, of course. Select the appropriate style for each situation and each individual. You wouldn't address your child, Lloyd, or one of your nurses, Janet, like an army recruit. You'd be much more gentle. But the principle's the same.

"Practice this step, and these reviews will, over time, get you into the habit of making constant small improvements.

"Okay. Now you have tools for establishing accountability. Fine. People are accountable. But accountable for what?"

Tony turned to the chalkboard and circled the word "GOALS."

"Goals help with two things in particular. First, they create a proactive rather than a reactive mindset. And second, they create a focus. Too many people fall into the 'activity trap.' They get so caught up in the activity that they lose sight of why they're doing it.

"Goals are what you expect to see accomplished by carrying out your action plans. And that's what you want people to be accountable for — reaching goals.

"Jack Welch was a master of this at GE. First of all, he set the goals high. He believed that you have a much greater capacity for accomplishing things than you normally use, greater than you can even see in yourself. In ways large and small, every part of his message — his words, his actions, his nonverbal cues — he communicated this belief, along with his high expectations for reaching the most ambitious goals."

"Tony," Mike broke in, "as you said, Welch set very high goals. That was in a very competitive business situation, where he was dealing with adults and everybody knew it was sink or swim. I don't feel I can do that in school. My responsibility is to help students learn, not make the school the biggest business in the country. Teachers don't have the option of hiring and firing students. If I set the goals too high, too many students will become demoralized, fail, give up, or drop out."

"Yes, of course you're right, Mike. That's why goals should be handled the same way as accountability — according to the situation and the individual. You don't treat school children the same way Carlos deals with production people or the way Janet handles her nursing staff. But the principles are basically the same.

"GE is still noted for its consistently high goals. One of the reasons those high goals work for GE is that its people are supported in reaching those goals. You can supply that needed support using a concept called 'gradient stress.' Let me illustrate." On the board, Tony quickly sketched a vertical scale:

"On this scale, 1 represents little stress and 8 to 10 represents the breaking point. If you have people at stress level 1 and you take them up to stress level 2, 3, or 4, you're stretching them. At stress level 5, 6, or 7, you're straining them — but if you give them the support they need to make the adjustment, they can handle it.

"If you go straight from level 1 to level 8, 9, or 10, you take them to the breaking point — which means that no matter how much support you give them, they won't be able to handle the stress. Too many leaders try to accomplish lofty goals without giving even a modest amount of support — and then they wonder why their people don't perform the way GE'ers do. You often see the same thing with firstborns, or eight-year-old Little Leaguers, or anyone of whom too much is expected without much support. They're stressed to the breaking point, and they fail, big time.

"Here's the key to using gradient stress to get the most out of others. Once someone has been at stress 5 and has grown comfortable at that level, it becomes that person's new level 1. Now the point that would have been stress level 9 or 10 becomes stress level 5 — which the person can handle with support from you. So a level of performance that might have seemed out of reach twelve months before becomes doable, as long as you provide the necessary support.

"That support comes from positive expectations, which we've discussed, and positive feedback, which we'll talk about later.

"Many companies set tough goals, it's true — quite often, tougher goals than many people think it's possible to reach. But the key thing in making it work is providing support.

"I find that companies that grow people grow profits. Companies that shrink people shrink profits. And the more support you put into the system, the faster you can grow people.

**The more support you put into the system, the faster you can grow people.**

"Teachers do the same thing, using a different style. They tell the student, 'I know you can do much better work than this. I know you have the capability, and so I want to help you do as well as you can.'

"Now, to answer your question, Mike, there are two schools of thought on how high to set goals. One view is that they should be set so high that people have to stretch to reach them. We know that setting ambitious goals can sometimes motivate people to overcome all obstacles and hit the target. But there's a danger that if goals are set too high, people will simply feel all efforts are futile and give up.

"The other school says that since success itself is motivating, goals should be set low enough that people are sure to reach them, and in reaching the goals they will be motivated, and that motivation will produce even better results in the future. The counterargument is that if the goal is too modest, there's no challenge, and people lose interest. Like playing tennis without a net, as the poet said.

"To me, there's some truth in both arguments, and the more reading I do in motivation and goal-setting research, the more I believe this. So I've come up with something I call the 'Inverted Motivation Curve' to summarize what I've found.

"It seems that if there's a 100 percent probability of success, there's not much motivation. And if there's no probability of success, there's also not much motivation. The maximum motivation seems to be in the area where there's a high probability of achieving some success but still some risk and challenge involved.

"The curve looks something like this." Tony quickly drew another diagram on the chalkboard:

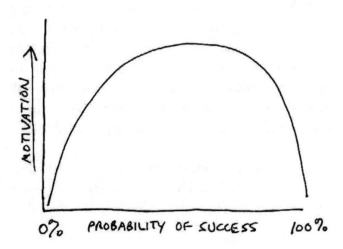

"Having given this a lot of thought, I prefer to suggest that the best way to set goals is to cover several bases at once. First, agree with the person on the minimum level of performance to be achieved in all areas; then set breakthrough goals for one to three of those areas. This provides both kinds of motivation: the satisfaction of meeting the easier goals and the challenge of trying to achieve the tougher ones.

"Let's take a parent and child as an example. Lloyd, suppose you're trying to get Lori to set her sights a little higher. Let's say she's getting all D's. You might say, 'How about if we agree that you will get at least a C in all your courses, and you'll shoot for a B in at least two subjects?' Or you might suggest that she aim for no less than 75 on all tests but at least 85 on two of her next five tests. This gives her some fairly easy targets and a few that are more challenging.

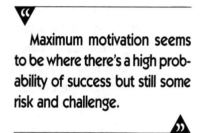

**Maximum motivation seems to be where there's a high probability of success but still some risk and challenge.**

"For another example, let's talk about sales. Mary, what metrics would you use to set goals with your sales reps? Sales volume? Number of new customers?"

Mary reflected for a moment. "I would say sales volume, gross margin percentage, average order size, and customer satisfaction would be the most useful."

"Let's make it a real-life example," said Tony. "Give us some numbers that might represent easy goals or minimal improvement."

Mary took a moment to write a few numbers on her note pad. "In my shop, I would say that a low target for a sales rep would be $100,000 a month in sales with an average order size of $3,000 and a gross margin of 20 percent. And a customer satisfaction rating above 4.0 on a five-point scale."

"Okay, now let's apply what we know from the Inverted Motivation Curve. First, you get the sales rep's agreement that these are reasonable goals — goals that he or she might expect to accomplish fairly easily. Then you ask — let's say we're talking about Marvin here — ask Marvin to choose two areas where he could really stretch himself. Let's say he picks sales volume and gross margin. You discuss these with him and perhaps get him to commit to $135,000 per month by the first of November. And he agrees to raise his gross margin from his current 19 percent to 22 percent by July 15.

"Just as Lloyd did with Lori, you've made it clear what results Marvin is accountable for. Lloyd, as long as Lori gets somewhere between 75 and 85 on her next five tests, you can tell her two things: first, she's having some success in her studies; second, there's room for improvement. Those are very important things to be able to tell someone.

"The same applies to Marvin. As long as he brings in between $100,000 and $135,000 a month and his gross margin runs between 20 and 22 percent, you give him support by praising his successes, while still encouraging him to keep improving toward the higher targets.

"**S**o, Mike, if your question is do we set goals high or low — my answer is yes." Mike and Janet laughed; the others smiled.

"I can't emphasize too strongly the importance of goals. Too often we find that individuals fail to perform as well as they could because they don't know what's expected of them. Leaders think they've communicated exactly what the person is expected to accomplish, but if you ask the team member or subordinate or student or child what he or she is accountable for, the answer might be quite different.

"Have any of you ever experienced this kind of misunderstanding?"

"You bet," said Carlos.

**Often people fail to perform as well as they could because they don't know what's expected of them.**

"Ten years ago, I worked for a guy who was always hopping all over me for not doing certain things. But they were things I didn't know I was supposed to be working on. Not knowing is like being sucker-punched in a fight you don't even know you're in. Ever since then, I've been very careful to let people know what I expect from them."

"That's exactly what you have to do. And here's an awareness test you can use to see how well you and the other person concur on the expected performance level. This is a very simple three-part test. It can work equally well for any of you. Let's read through it together." Tony handed everyone a single page:

---

AWARENESS TEST

1. On a single sheet of paper, write the answers to the following questions about a key team member, child, or student:

   a. What are the key areas of responsibility or account-ability for this individual?

   b. In each of these key areas, what are the critical metrics or performance indicators that should be used to measure results?

   c. For each indicator, specify the performance level you expect the person to achieve and the date by which you think it should be achieved.

2. Without revealing your own responses, ask the team member, child, or student to answer the same three questions.

3. Compare your responses. If they don't match, you have a problem. It's unlikely that person can or will perform as you expect.

---

"Oh, I think I see what you mean, Tony," said Janet excitedly. "So if I want improved teamwork, I not only need to identify teamwork as a key area we're account-able for, I also need to lay out the measurements on how we'll decide whether or not we have teamwork."

"Yes, and I think you'll find that keeping track of a few key indicators helps keep other actions running smoother, too. In sales, for instance, if your rep meets a quota in improving monthly sales volume, chances are that person's average order size will go up, too.

"Over the years, lots of people have taken this test in all kinds of organizations and at all levels. When we surveyed the results, we found that the person administering the test and the person taking the test answered the questions differently about 25 percent of the time. We looked into these cases and found that seldom had there been any detailed discussion of goals. No one had agreed on specific areas of responsibility; no one had talked about how to measure performance or what the goal was or when it was to be reached.

"The implications are pretty serious. If you don't agree on what constitutes success, how can it be achieved? How can you be an effective leader if the people you're leading don't know what they're accountable for? Maybe one reason the school committee you're on isn't making any progress is because no one has been given the responsibility or been assigned specific accountabilities that would make the progress possible. Maybe one reason your production teams aren't achieving higher quality, Carlos, is because you and they have a different picture of what that quality looks like or how it's measured.

"The reason someone isn't doing his best is rarely willful negligence — it's usually simple misunderstanding. The person doesn't know what's expected. Exhorting him to do his best when he's not sure what his 'best' is doesn't do much good. It may only make him work harder toward the wrong goals.

"Now, you'll notice that I've already started talking about the next ingredient in accountability." Picking up a piece of chalk, he circled the words "DEVELOP ACTION PLANS."

"Action plans — as I mentioned — are the insurance that you'll reach your goal. Action plans spell out all the steps, large and small, that must be taken to meet overall objectives, like the bricks needed to complete the room you're adding on. Think of your action plan as both the road map to your chosen destination and your method of getting there.

"In baseball, a player might set a goal to raise his batting average from last season's .275 to .325. Action steps might include spending at least an hour a day in the batting cage, getting feedback from the batting coach, spending more time analyzing opposing pitchers, and increased weight training. Of course, you would spell out each of these steps in more detail than I did just now.

"In sales, your goal might be a 25 percent overall improvement in revenue; your action steps might include targeting five high-potential accounts, identifying current accounts where there's an opportunity for substantially more business, creating a sales call plan for each of these accounts, and setting up a telephone call plan for all accounts under a certain size.

"For a student, the goal of improving by one letter grade overall might include studying longer, studying at a different place or time of day, spending more time — or less time — studying in groups, or taking on more extra-credit assignments — again, more specifically than I've just outlined here.

"Now, here's one more question to ponder. We've talked about establishing accountability, selecting goals, and developing action plans. All of these are done in dialog with the individuals whose performance you want to enhance. To what idea does this naturally lead us?"

Once more, Tony turned to the board. He circled the word "ENGAGE."

"The more engaged people are in the development of goals, plans, and feedback, the more accountable they become. Let me illustrate.

"In one manufacturing company I worked with, quality control and manufacturing were constantly at war with each other. The quality department conducted daily audits of overall plant quality and ascribed defects to individual departments. But none of these departments wanted to believe the reports. Instead, they complained: 'Those quality jerks think this place is run so they can point out defects.' 'All they want to do is shut the line down.' 'You can audit a product right down to nothing if you keep looking for defects the way those idiots do.' In other words, a lot of the organization's energy was directed toward trying to prove that the other guy was wrong.

"So we changed the feedback system to increase the employees' sense of engagement. We had individuals audit their own performance continuously. A supervisor and one of the hourly rated employees would spot check five or six products from their own work group, using the same criteria that quality assurance was using. Within a week, things began to improve. As people checked not only their own work but that of their peers and colleagues, they began to see how product quality could be improved. They saw defects they had missed before, and what's more important, they began to accept responsibility for defects. Team leaders and hourly employees who had complained about quality control began to work on improving quality on their own.

"When I asked one of the hourly employees why he thought quality was improving, he said, 'Quality control used to take units off the line, look at them, mark everything that was wrong, and send the department head a note that said what a lousy job we had done. The department head would go yell at the supervisor. The supervisor had to yell at someone, so he'd turn and yell at us. I think most of the defects they found happened further down the line — you know, people dropping or scratching the product. Most of them were probably caused by someone else and just charged back to us because everybody hates us. This new system's pretty good, though. We take turns, and every day a different person goes around with the team leader and checks

'We can tell right away how we're running, and if something isn't right, we can correct it.'

the products. This way we can tell right away how we're running, and if something isn't right, we can correct it. We know when things are right and when they're wrong because we're doing the checking ourselves. The truth of the matter is we know more about making a quality product than those guys in the quality department.'

"So by involving workers directly in the quality control effort," Tony continued, "we increased their engagement. This principle is crucial in building accountability into any job. When students, nurses, sales reps, team members, or others are engaged in setting their own goals, developing action plans to achieve goals, and providing their own feedback, they become more accountable for producing good results. This is true in the workplace, at school, or in the home.

"This doesn't mean that as teacher, team leader, parent, or company president you have to let everyone set his or her own goals. You may have to pick the overall targets yourself, or assign an executive team to do most of the strategic target setting, then work in a more collegial fashion to engage everyone else in the effort. Your ratio of telling to asking depends on the situation, the people involved, and your leadership style.

"If you have team members or an executive staff or students who are already highly motivated, you'll almost always find that they will set higher targets for themselves than you would ever dream of setting. All you have to do is get out of the way and watch them succeed.

"Even people who are performing far beneath their potential may set higher goals than you would set for them. Sometimes these lower performers will set goals so high that they're not really engaged. That's where the Inverted Motivation Curve can be useful. Acknowledge the over-ambitious goal, then ask them what goal would be one they're absolutely sure they'll hit. Then you'll have the high-low effect, which will increase their commitment.

"At times you may have to get more directly involved in spelling out the goals. When you do, let them take the lead in developing action plans to reach the goals. If you're talking with a student, Mike, you might say, 'Billy, what needs to be done to get a score of at least ninety on two of your next five tests?' Then you and Billy work out the necessary steps. Mary, when you're talking with either Marvin or Pat, you can ask him to figure out — or you can figure out together — the steps to increase sales and gross margin percentage at the same time.

"Y̶ou hear a lot about creativity and brainstorming, right? This is where it happens — in action planning. There's nothing particularly creative about setting the goals. The creativity comes in laying out the action plan that will help you reach those goals. And so that there's no way anybody can misunderstand, don't forget to put your action plan on paper.

"Do people really want to be held that accountable for things?" asked Janet.

"Probably some don't, but most do. The message I get from people regarding accountability is 'Let me know what you want me to do, hold me accountable for getting results, and then get out of my way.'"

"Well, that's certainly the way I like to be managed, so I guess that would apply to others," said Janet.

"Not as exciting as talking about high expectations, is it?" There was a murmur of agreement, and Tony continued, "No mystery or magic to it, that's for sure. Compared with getting others energized, motivated, and excited about reaching goals or praising their good work, holding them accountable is kind of a downer. But it's a crucial part of bringing out their best.

> **"**
> **The message I get from people is 'Let me know what you want me to do, hold me accountable for getting results, and then get out of my way.'**
> **》**

"Okay, let's break for lunch," said Tony. "Feed yourselves well, because this afternoon we're going to talk about the last of the three elements: feedback."

# Feedback

## *The Focus of Self-Awareness*

"Feedback. We all know what that means, don't we? Feedback is information we receive that tells us how well we're doing. We turn the steering wheel, and we can see and feel the car going around the curve. We take an exam in school, and we see how well we're learning the subject matter. Feedback helps us stay on track and make progress toward the goal.

"But as you'll discover, feedback comes in many forms. We're going to talk about three basic types of feedback that are essential in bringing out the best in others. These three types are motivational feedback, informational feedback, and developmental feedback.

"Not long ago, in a sales leadership workshop for a pharmaceutical firm, I was describing the difference between motivational feedback and informational feedback. Motivational feedback, I said, is cheering a football team. Informational feedback is like the yard-line markers — it gives both the players and the fans a way of measuring progress toward the goal line. Information is good, but it's not enough. It's the clapping and cheering that does the most to motivate the players.

"At that point, one of the workshop participants said, 'You know, you just helped me understand something that's been puzzling me. About three months ago, during a meeting with my district sales managers, I asked them to lock themselves in a room for two or three hours and figure out what they wanted me to do, stop doing, or do differently to help them in their jobs. One of the things they said they wanted from me was more feedback. I couldn't believe it! I have meetings with them; I talk to them on the phone; I go over reports with them in person; I travel with them; I pass along market information from headquarters; I forward e-mail to them. If anything, I thought I was overloading them with feedback.

"'But what you just said about different kinds of feedback opened my eyes. They didn't want more information — they wanted more motivation! They want me to tell them they're doing a good job. All I was doing was sharing information with them, and although that's certainly an important part of my job, it's also important to use that information as a basis for reinforcement when it shows that someone is doing a good job.'"

Tony went on: "Then he asked me what developmental feedback was. I explained that it was corrective action taken when someone isn't performing up to standard — the head of a department whose quality isn't where it should be, a sales rep whose sales need to be 10 or 15 percent higher, a student whose grades aren't as good as they could be.

"This is where you use 'supportive confrontation of nonperformance.' You have to confront nonperformance, but you need to do it in a way that creates commitment rather than grudging compliance or outright resistance.

> **You have to confront nonperformance, but you need to do it in a way that creates commitment rather than grudging compliance or outright resistance.**

"All three forms of feedback are important. Using one without the others doesn't do much good. And that's why we're going to spend most of the afternoon examining all three."

# 6

# Motivational Feedback
## *Accelerating Improvement*

"A minute ago I compared motivational feedback to the cheering a football team gets when it's gaining yardage. But even when results are positive, motivational feedback can generally take any of three basic forms. The fans may cheer wildly and vigorously; they might boo if they are less than pleased with results; or they can sit on their hands and act as though nothing has happened.

"The same thing can happen in other performance fields. If a sales rep shows an improvement in performance, we might acknowledge her for it; we might criticize her and say she should have done even better; or we might do and say nothing. The same is true with a child learning to sing a song, or a student learning to write better book reports, or a work team improving product quality, or any person or persons making some progress toward a goal. It's a common occurrence:

someone engages in appropriate behavior and receives either positive feedback, negative feedback, or no feedback at all."

Tony stopped talking. He was sitting now, with his feet propped up on an empty chair. A mischievous grin played across his face. He looked around the room. "This morning someone told me the greatest joke. Anybody want to hear it?"

The others grinned back at Tony and nodded. "Go for it!" said Lloyd.

"I don't know if I can tell it," said Tony, shaking his head. "I laugh every time I think of it." He started chuckling to himself. Soon he was laughing out loud, turning his face away from them and shielding his eyes with his hand. Most of his students were laughing, too, amused — and not a little puzzled.

"Wait a minute, wait a minute," he said, stifling his laugh. "This is embarrassing. I can't stop laughing long enough to tell it. Anybody else got a joke to tell?"

The laughing stopped and room grew quiet. They were still smiling, but for a minute no one spoke.

Then Mike said, "Okay, there were these two hobos — "

"Wait," Tony interrupted. "I don't want to start laughing again. Once I get started I can't stop. Let's do it this way. Each of you write down the funniest joke you can think of on a sheet of paper and hand it to me.

The shorter, the better. Put your name at the top. I'll give you a minute."

Mike, Lloyd, and Janet started writing almost immediately. Mary looked around anxiously; Carlos scratched his chin. Then both began scribbling.

"Hand them to me when you finish," said Tony, smiling. "I want to see them before we tell them to each other, okay?" Looking dubious, they complied.

Tony read the topmost joke. Suddenly he broke out laughing. "That's a great one, Janet! Thanks! Hold on a minute and you can tell the others. They'll fall over laughing!" Janet grinned broadly.

Tony looked at the next sheet of paper, read silently, then frowned. "Mike, I don't think you quite understood me. This one isn't very funny. Sorry. Maybe you should try again." He handed the sheet back to Mike, who turned noticeably red but said nothing.

"Let's see what you wrote, Carlos." Tony read Carlos's paper. His facial expression did not change. When he finished reading, he put Carlos's paper on the table and said nothing. Ignoring Carlos, he looked at Mary. "Well, let's look at Mary's joke." Again he read silently, saying nothing, betraying no response, then placed Mary's joke on the table alongside Carlos's.

He picked up the last joke — Lloyd's — and read it to himself. The tension grew in the room. As before, he said nothing — just put down the paper and sat staring at them without expression. After a few endless seconds, he broke into a grin, then began laughing harder and harder. The others, all except Mike, began to smile nervously.

Quite suddenly, Tony stopped laughing and said, "Quick, somebody tell me what I'm doing."

After a moment, Janet and Mary shouted, in unison: "Feedback!"

"Exactly!" said Tony. "I just gave you three kinds of motivational feedback. And I'll let you in on a secret: I lied.

"I didn't read your jokes. I only pretended to read them. For all I know, each one is funnier than the last. Doesn't matter. What matters is the feedback I gave you.

"Janet, you seemed happy when I laughed and complimented your joke. Made you feel good, didn't it?"

"Yes, it did," she grinned. "Now I can only hope it's as funny as you pretended it was."

"Well, later we'll pass them around and you can all decide for yourselves. But the positive feedback I gave you made you feel, at least for a second or two, like a stand-up comic, didn't it? Come on, admit it!"

"Almost. That's all I'll say," laughed Janet.

"And Mike. My response kind of irritated you, didn't it?"

"Well . . . yes, I guess it did. I'm glad you weren't serious, because it was pretty darned good, if I have to say so myself."

"It probably was. I honestly don't know. I was just demonstrating negative feedback. But when I criticized you and asked you to try again, did you at least get a momentary urge to 'show me'?"

"Yes, I did," grinned Mike. "Right after my urge to deck you."

They laughed. Tony said, "What about you, Carlos? What feelings did you have after I 'read' — quote unquote — your joke?"

"Well, I was disappointed, of course. I felt like — like my joke was so bad it didn't even deserve a response. To tell you the truth, I felt disrespect. Mike got criticized, but I didn't even rate that much. It definitely was not a good feeling."

"Did you feel angry about it?"

"Not angry so much as — well, kind of in limbo. I didn't know whether to be mad or maybe feel guilty because my joke was so bad, or what."

"Did you feel energized?"

"No," said Carlos. "It kind of left me feeling drained and confused. Not knowing how to react."

"It was the same for me, Tony," said Mary. "I couldn't figure out what was going on. It didn't seem like you. I thought for a second I had done something terribly wrong."

"Would you have preferred the way I came down on Mike?" asked Tony.

"Well . . . yes, I think so. At least then I'd have known where I stood. And how to feel about it."

"Wait a minute, Tony," said Lloyd. "You mean my joke stunk?" Everyone laughed.

"I have a confession to make, Lloyd." Tony paused.

"I read yours. I tried not to laugh, but I couldn't help myself." They all laughed, and Lloyd looked pleased.

"Here's the point I was demonstrating," said Tony. He turned and wrote on the board:

POSITIVE FEEDBACK = REINFORCEMENT

"Positive feedback is energizing. It validates your efforts. It makes you feel you've accomplished something, and it makes you want to achieve even greater things. Everybody has experienced this, and everybody knows it works. That's why good leaders naturally use positive feedback as reinforcement whenever they can."

Again he turned to the board:

NEGATIVE FEEDBACK = PUNISHMENT

"Negative feedback is also energizing, but in a different way. When somebody is told, *in a negative manner,* that he's fallen short of what's expected of him, he's being punished. The result is often a renewed effort to perform better, but not always. Some leaders use negative feedback when performance has improved, if it hasn't improved as much as the leader wanted it to. Sometimes this works, but often it only makes the person feel as if he's being punished for trying. And people who are consistently punished for trying will what? That's right, they'll eventually stop trying."

Finally, Tony wrote:

## NO FEEDBACK = EXTINCTION

"The third kind of motivational feedback is extinction — that is, no feedback at all. Extinction, as you have seen, is even more punishing than negative feedback. It's the least motivating response you can make to any action. Obviously, if you ignore somebody's truly bad performance, as if it didn't happen, that poor performance is likely to be repeated or even grow worse. Not so obviously, if you make no response whatsoever to someone's good performance, even a marginal improvement, you're going to extinguish her motivation to do better. She's put in extra effort to improve, but it hasn't been recognized.

"Now let me ask you: which of these is our most common type of feedback for improved performance? You guessed it — extinction.

"All of us like attention. If we can't get good attention, then we'll settle for bad attention. The thing we find hardest to accept is no attention.

"Which raises the question: Why do so many of us, as leaders, seem to get things backwards? We're overattentive and quick to criticize when someone messes up. Sometimes we offer praise when outstanding performance catches our attention. But worst of all, when someone does something well, or when someone performs reliably all the time, or when someone works hard and makes steady progress, we often say and do nothing at all.

> **Most of us are woefully unaware of extinction and how devastating it can be.**

"Most of us know the difference between reinforcement and punishment. But most of us are woefully unaware of extinction and how devastating it can be.

"If you remember nothing else, I want you to leave here with one principle in mind: Bringing out the best in others requires that we reinforce improvements, even if they're not 'there' yet.

> **Bringing out the best in others requires that we reinforce improvements, even if they're not 'there' yet.**

"Why is this so? Because once you get a behavior pattern started, it takes only a small amount of reinforcement to keep it going. A habit is like a car; it's hard to start it moving, but once it's rolling down the highway, all it takes is a little push on the gas pedal now and then to keep it going. But if you stop giving it gas altogether, it will eventually stop rolling. And if you stop reinforcing desirable behavior altogether, that behavior will eventually stop — unless, of course, it's being reinforced from somewhere else."

Carlos said, "Tony, unless I'm missing something here, I have a problem with what you're saying. I can't see supervisors walking up and down the line saying, 'Ooooo, that's a very nice batch of paper you just ran.' They'd get laughed out of the plant."

"I would agree," said Tony. "Reinforcement has to fit the time, the place, the event, and the person. Reinforcement that's appropriate for one person in one situation may not be appropriate at all for another individual in the same situation or for the same person under different circumstances.

"Positive reinforcement is not about hearts and flowers and just being nice to people. It's about giving them feedback that makes them want to keep doing what they're doing. Remember the Ranger instructor I mentioned earlier? He had the same question. And my answer to him was similar to the answer I'm going to give you. I told him to use positive reinforcement more frequently, but in a much tougher manner with his soldiers than he would use if he were leading civilians — in a hospital staff or a classroom, for example.

What if a supervisor went up to someone on the line and said, 'Joe, I just want you to know that your good work has not gone unnoticed. You're one of our best operators, and we appreciate the key role you play in keeping up quality and productivity.' Or if it's someone he's known for many years, he might say, 'Frank, you're the sorriest-looking S.O.B. in the shop, but no one would know that from your work. You're doing a great job with throughput and productivity. Keep it up!' If it's someone who is easily embarrassed by being singled out in public, rather than being cornered on the shop floor he could get a personal note in his mailbox — or if he has a bonus coming, a note in his pay envelope."

"Okay, that makes sense," said Carlos. "I've given bonuses before, but adding a note of thanks is a nice touch. I'll try that next time."

"Don't let too much time go by, Carlos. That's my next point, and it's the first of five principles I want to present to you about giving positive reinforcement. We'll cover all five, then take a little break. In case you'd like to write them down, I'll put them on the board now."

1. Reinforce immediately.

2. Reinforce ANY improvement, not just excellence.

3. Reinforce specifically.

4. Reinforce new behaviors continuously.

5. Reinforce good habits intermittently.

"As I was saying to Carlos: to be most effective, reinforcement should follow performance as closely as possible. The more immediate it is, the more powerful. Too often, positive feedback happens a day, a week, a month, six months, or a year after the behavior it is supposed to reinforce. When this happens, it doesn't have much effect on behavior. It might make you feel good to give it, and it might make the recipient feel good, but it doesn't do much to get the individual to continue that behavior.

"This is why performance reviews seldom have any permanent impact on an individual's behavior. They're simply too far removed in time. Sure, they might generate a quick rush of pride — or if they're negative, chagrin — but the effect is short-lived. If Joan does a good job of putting together a report on Tuesday, it doesn't do much good to wait four weeks to tell her. Tell her on Tuesday or Wednesday, when the report is still fresh in her mind, and in yours.

"The same thing applies to grades, Mike. By the time his report card comes out, a student should already know approximately what that report card is going to look like — because you should be providing real-time feedback along the way. Remember, too, that the report card is just informational feedback; what you need to give day-to-day is motivational feedback. When you hand back a test paper with a B-plus on it, you should say, 'Dave, I noticed that your spelling is getting better. That shows a lot of hard work on your part. Keep it up.'

"Janet, immediate feedback might be saying to one of your first-shift nurses, 'Peg, I noticed that you're providing that little extra bit of information that helps the second shift get set up and running with the patients. That's good thinking.'

"Lloyd, for you it means noticing the things your daughter is doing right — even if her grades aren't as good as they should be — and reinforcing those behaviors as they are occurring. For example, if you see her studying, you might say, 'Lori, it looks like you're putting in more time studying and doing your homework. That's terrific, because that's the kind of hard work that will make a difference. It might help you on your very next test, but even if it doesn't, I know it will pay off in the end.'

"Saying this to Lori registers on two levels. First, the cognitive level: Lori makes an intellectual connection between what she's doing and the impact on either short-term scores or her final grade. Second, on the unconscious level, Lori associates studying with a positive event — the reinforcement. This is where habit formation occurs, and by praising her behavior you are reinforcing the formation of good habits.

"Lloyd, you may have noticed that what I just said has some of the second principle in it, too: reinforce improvement as well as excellence. This is especially important when you're trying to overcome bad habits and replace them with good habits.

"The problem, as I said earlier, is that we usually do a pretty good job of reinforcing excellence, but a poor job of reinforcing simple improvements. We make a big deal out of making all-state quarterback, and we let Lori know how pleased we are when she gets an A-plus on a test, and when teamwork between departments is really outstanding, we comment on it. But we don't say much, if anything, to the guy who's making progress but still isn't quite doing the job we want him to. It doesn't come naturally to us.

"Lloyd, let's say that Lori gets mostly D's and you'd like to see her getting B's and C's. Is there a course where she's consistently getting D's?"

"Yes," said Lloyd. "She usually gets D's in math."

"Has she ever gotten a C on any math assignment or test?"

"She almost never gets a C."

"Does she *ever* get a C?" Tony persisted.

"Well, occasionally," said Lloyd.

"When was the last time?"

"About a month ago, I think."

"And exactly what did you do?"

Lloyd was silent as he sat looking down at the table. Then he shook his head and said, "I didn't do anything."

"Do you see what you're doing?" asked Tony.

"Yes, I do. What's that term you used? Extinction?"

"That's it exactly. You were extinguishing her improvements. Extinction is our most common response, *and* it's our most devastating response."

> **Extinction is our most common response, *and* it's our most devastating response.**

"Then what I should do," said Lloyd, "is whenever I see even a slight improvement, compliment Lori?"

"Yes. And you can discuss with her what she did differently to improve. If she's finding it easier to get up early and study before class, tell her you'll help by getting up earlier to fix breakfast or take her to school before classes begin so she can use the school library. Support her good decisions, and encourage her to make more good decisions."

"I guess I'm guilty of the same thing," said Mary. "When I have a heart-to-heart with Marvin, it's usually because his performance has slipped below par again. So I should talk with him, compliment him, every time I notice even a slight improvement?"

"Essentially, yes," said Tony. "Tell him you appreciate the effort he's putting into his work. Tell him what a good role model he makes for the newer reps."

"Tony, I would love to be able to do what you're suggesting," said Mike. "But I have twenty-eight students in my class. Spending just three minutes with each student would take an hour and a half every day. How can I possibly give encouragement to every student every day?"

"Yes, your job is uniquely difficult, Mike, because you're not encouraging students to learn as a means of reaching a corporate goal. Your goal is learning for its own sake, and every student represents a unique set of personal goals.

"But immediate feedback doesn't necessarily mean instantaneous or face-to-face feedback. If a test score is noticeably above par for a student, write a complimentary note on the paper before returning it, highlighting its strengths. Other teachers have found it easiest to build feedback into other tasks, such as grading papers or just day-to-day comments.

"The other key thing is to remember to reinforce improvements. In my experience, teachers, like everybody else, are good with feedback for outstanding work but somewhat lax in reinforcing steady improvement. If you want more improvement, you have to reinforce improvement.

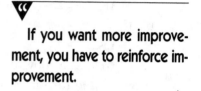

**If you want more improvement, you have to reinforce improvement.**

"Just remember, even though it's best to give positive reinforcement face-to-face, it's not always possible. Some of you may find it more practical at times to give feedback over the phone or by voice mail or e-mail."

T he room fell silent for a moment. Tony looked at Carlos. "Carlos, you look skeptical."

"I'm still not sure I buy into all of this," said Carlos. "Look. I pay people to do a good job, so they should do a good job. Shouldn't that paycheck be reinforcement enough? I ask my managers to turn in reports that are complete, concise, and well-organized. They understand that it's part of their job. I'm paying them to turn in good reports; I expect them to turn in good reports. Why should I go out of my way to compliment them for doing what they're getting paid to do?"

"Does everybody turn in good reports?" asked Tony.

"No, some of the reports could stand some improvement."

"Are the people who turn in poor reports getting paid?"

"Yes."

"Well," said Tony, "it sounds like you're paying some people *not* to turn in good reports."

"No, no," said Carlos. "I guess I didn't say it clearly. I'm paying them to turn in good reports. It's just that they're not turning in good reports."

"Step back from your personal involvement in the situation, Carlos, and let's look at it another way. From a behavioral point of view, two things are happening: number one, people are turning in reports that are less than satisfactory, and number two, they are getting paid. So, behaviorally, you are, in effect, paying them for not turning in good reports."

Carlos was silent for a minute. "I don't like that," he said. "But you're right. That's exactly what I'm doing."

Tony looked at the others. "We all do it," he said. "We don't intend to, but we do. And yet virtually everyone likes positive reinforcement in some form.

"**M**ost of us need or appreciate a pat on the back, at least once in a while. And people who are making an effort to do things better deserve all the encouragement you can give them."

Tony paused, then went on: "Now, let's suppose you're sitting face-to-face with someone who's writing reports for you. This person's work has its high points and low points, and you've got to discuss the pluses and the minuses.

"You could say, 'Bob, this report is pretty good overall, but it still needs some work. Thanks for coming in.' But that would be a waste of time, wouldn't it? It might make you feel better, but you didn't give Bob any useful feedback. Instead, he will leave feeling confused and uncertain about how to improve the report. You haven't given him any specifics. This is no better than just walking past him in the hall and saying, 'Adequate job, Bob!'

"What do most supervisors do in this situation? Usually, their tendency is to mention what's good in general terms and be more specific about the faults. As in: 'Overall, you did a good job on the report, Bob, but the lead paragraph didn't tell us enough about the subject, and your conclusion wasn't clear about your most important finding. Oh yeah, one other thing — you need to work on your punctuation.'

"Here are some other variations you've probably heard:

"'Well, I'm glad you got the order, Molly, but are you sure you didn't leave any money on the table by giving ground on the price? And are you sure they'll come back and reorder from us? If they don't, we won't make much on this deal.'

"Or, 'The three C's are nice, Ben, but you still have two D's to work on.'

"And one of my all-time favorites: 'That's a nice tie, Tony. Are those coming back into style?'"

When the laughter stopped, Tony continued: "There are two major problems with this approach. First, not only are you not giving enough informational feedback, you're probably providing negative motivational feedback, even though you started with a compliment.

"You're hurting motivation because you're conditioning the individual to wait for the other shoe to drop. After hearing 'It's good, but . . .' time after time, people stop hearing the positives and just brace themselves for whatever comes after the 'but.' Eventually, because they fear the hidden barb, they become unresponsive to compliments and immune to reinforcement.

"Your interactions become basically negative. This taints all your relationships with others. People begin to assume that every interaction with you will be unpleasant. They will avoid you. And you can't help someone develop his full potential if you can't interact with him.

"The second thing is that although people learn quickly what's wrong with their work, they never find out what's right with it. Since they don't know what they did right, they have no model to follow, so they don't learn how to capitalize on their strengths. They have nothing to emulate the next time they do the work. They will never become self-sufficient but will always depend on others for guidance.

"How do you avoid this? By being just as specific about what's right with the work as what's wrong with it. Like this: 'Overall, you did a good job on the report, Bob. Let's go through it pretty much section by section. The first section doesn't tell us enough about the subject, and your conclusion isn't clear about the most important finding, which you actually handled very well in the third section The second and fourth sections are especially useful. I like the way you summarize the potential downsides and outline some possible contingency plans to counteract them. And the list of alternate contacts will be very useful if we go ahead with our expansion plans. The third section is probably the best of all. It has the same level of detail that sections two and four have, and as you can see from my notes, the clarity is outstanding.'"

Janet raised her hand and asked, "Tony, what do you do when someone's work has more bad than good in it? Do you talk about the good stuff first, then go into the bad stuff? Or is it better to try to go back and forth between the good and the bad?"

"The best way to handle that situation is much like the way I did in the last example. Review the work section by section — but in the normal order. Whether it's a student, a sales rep, an executive, or a nurse, if you put a lot of energy into deciding which section to discuss first, that person's going to waste a lot more energy trying to figure out why you selected the order you did."

"This is beginning to sound like a lot of work," said Mary. "Are you saying we have to provide reinforcement constantly, day after day and week after week, to keep someone motivated?"

"Not at all, Mary, and that brings me to the fourth and fifth principles of positive reinforcement. There are actually two main types of reinforcement schedules: continuous and intermittent. In continuous feedback, the individual is reinforced for virtually everything she does right or for almost every step she takes in the right direction. Intermittent feedback happens more or less randomly, like the payoff from a slot machine.

"Continuous reinforcement is best for developing new behaviors. You might use it with new employees or a student who's working at improving his skills. However, once somebody has reached a good, solid level of performance, you can switch to intermittent reinforcement. You might think, 'If reinforcement is good, then more of it is better.' But that's not really the case. More is better only when you're trying to build momentum.

"Once people get to a certain level of performance, they begin to reinforce themselves. A good sales rep knows when she walks out of the sales call whether she's done a good job. She can usually critique the positives and negatives of her own performance. All she needs from you is an occasional affirmation of her value to the company, and maybe some special attention when she's done a really outstanding job.

"I play tennis, and when I make a particularly good serve, I tell myself, 'Great serve!' However, it took an awful lot of reinforcement from my instructor on where to place my feet, how high to toss the ball, where to toss the ball, where to start the swing with the racquet, the follow-through, the move into the court, and a thousand and one other things I needed to get me to the point where I'm able to say to myself, 'Good serve, Tony.'

"And like most dedicated tennis nuts, I continue to take lessons. Why? Because, although I'll never be a great tennis player, I can always be a better tennis

> **Not everyone can be great, but everyone can be better. Our job is to help people improve.**

player. I suspect that's true of many of the people on your sales team, Mary, and on your nursing staff, Janet. And it's probably true of the managers and line workers in your company, Carlos, as well as your students, Mike. And the same will be true of your daughter, Lloyd, after she has built good study habits and is making steady progress. Not everyone can be great, but everyone can be better. Our job is to help people improve.

"If somebody is performing below what you consider an acceptable level, get face-to-face with him and reinforce him continually, real-time. Stick with it. Reinforce every improvement he makes, however small. Once he's performing well, back off and let momentum do the work — but surprise him with a good word or a pat on the back now and then."

# 7

# Informational Feedback

## *Roadmap to Success*

After the break, as everyone drifted back into the conference room, Tony wrote on the board:

GOAL-RELATED

IMMEDIATE

GRAPHIC

"Now we'll spend just a few minutes talking about the second type of feedback. We won't need a lot of time, because most of you are familiar with this kind of feedback, in one form or another.

"Informational feedback is simply what it says — providing information on performance. In school, it can come from keeping track of test scores in a single course or from recording all grades of any kind in all subjects. In sales, the metrics on which informational feedback can be based include sales volume, new accounts, customer satisfaction, gross margin, and average order size.

"As a rule, it's best to have the individual measure and monitor her own performance. She's more likely to believe the information if she keeps track of it herself, especially if her performance is below par. She can also react faster to correct the problem, because she can spot it before you do. This encourages self-management.

"Three things to keep in mind," said Tony, pointing to the board. "First, feedback should be goal-related.

"A goal is a powerful motivator. Mary, if you've already established a goal — or even better, a set of low and high goals — a sales rep will naturally have those targets in mind, so the informational feedback is simply a way to let him know what kind of progress he's making toward the target. Mike, if you and your student have agreed on a target of all test scores above 80 with at least two scores above 85, then you would naturally keep track of test scores.

"Second, informational feedback should be immediate. The problem with report cards, Mike, is that they give feedback anywhere from one week to one semester after the behavior being graded. The same goes for annual performance reviews, Carlos, where the lag time can be a whole year. That's why these feedback methods don't usually bring lasting behavioral changes.

"Whatever informational feedback system you set up, the information cycle should match the associated behavior. For instance, on an inside order desk, sales occur throughout the day, so you'll probably want to provide hourly feedback. The same goes for most production jobs. With grades, let the student know as soon as each test or paper is graded, if possible. And don't wait until the weekend to grade things. Grade them right away — certainly within one or two days for most things, although term papers or complex tests might take a little longer.

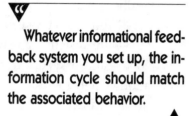

Whatever informational feedback system you set up, the information cycle should match the associated behavior.

"The third thing I want to emphasize is this: a picture is worth a thousand words. That's a cliché, but it's especially true in this case. A graph can give an instantaneous readout of progress. It has much more impact than a number. It can show both the specifics and the big picture at the same time. By putting grades on a graph, you can help a student see not only where she's been, but her current grade and her trend line. Graphs of sales volume, average order size, and so forth, can give a sales rep a snapshot of his performance. People don't always 'get' numbers, but most understand images right away, and one 'snapshot' of a graph can stick with them a long time."

"Help!" squeaked Janet. "Graph nurse cooperation by the hour? What about communication? Attitude? How am I even going to begin to do that?"

"Doesn't seem fair, does it? Of course, you're right, Janet. Your information is not 'hard' data like production line units or sales — so in your case, informational feedback may not be the best thing to use.

"You could try keeping track of progress for yourself — for instance, a private tally of the times you see good teamwork, such as nurses cooperating or helping another staff member. This will tell you if the motivational feedback you're providing is making a difference.

"If you did want to involve the nurses in your efforts, you could try establishing some sort of joint metric. For example, you could call a meeting to discuss your concerns about the lack of teamwork between shifts, then ask your nurses to rate current teamwork on a scale of one to ten. Over the next week, pay particular attention to everyone's teamwork behavior and reinforce even the slightest improvement. Then hold another meeting and ask everyone to rate teamwork again. Graph the results for everyone to see. Discuss the progress that's being made. Ask for ideas on how teamwork could be further improved. With everybody's attention focused on teamwork concerns and graphic evidence showing progress, this kind of subjective informational feedback can be made to serve as a basis for motivational feedback. It's not hard data like sales or units coming off a production line, but by getting everyone involved in measuring factors that are somewhat intangible, you can make it more objective."

# Developmental Feedback

*Course Corrections*

"Okay, I have to ask something," said Carlos. "I can see where all this stuff about positive expectations and reinforcement and accountability makes sense. And I see where I haven't been doing enough of that. But at some point, if an individual is not performing, you have to get hard-nosed about it. You have to sit down with him, face-to-face, and tell him he's got a problem. You can't be positive all the time. Everything you've said up to this point assumes that this person is making some effort to improve. What if he isn't? Or what if he seems to be making an effort but there's not much progress?"

"Good question, Carlos. That's the next topic on the agenda, so if nobody has any more questions about informational feedback, we can proceed. Anybody?"

Janet raised her hand. "Speaking of informational feedback, when do we get to see everybody's jokes?" This got a big laugh from everyone.

Tony picked up a sheaf of papers clipped together. "I had my assistant compile them and print them out on a single sheet. I'll pass them out before our next break. If I gave them to you now, we wouldn't get any work done."

He hesitated. "They're pretty good, actually. Couple of groaners, maybe. You can judge for yourself — later.

"For now, though, the subject is developmental feedback. And Carlos, since you brought it up, let's do a little role playing."

"Let's see. I ask a question and then I have to be in a role play. Is this an example of punishing good behavior?" asked Carlos with a smile.

Tony chuckled. "You'll enjoy it, Carlos. You can play yourself, and I'll be your production manager."

"Good. I think I can handle that," said Carlos.


"Okay, you start. I've just arrived in your office. You're concerned because product quality has been slipping and that affects productivity."

"All right. Tony, I've been looking over the production records for the past three months, and I see that the scrap rate has gone from 1.28 percent to 2.37 percent. What's going on? Why are we suddenly having to throw away more product?"

"Carlos, I can understand your disappointment, and I'm disappointed too, but the truth is that during that last production cutback we lost several key personnel, and we're having trouble hiring good replacements. That's part of it. The other thing is that quality control is being unreasonable. I think two of their line inspectors have it in for us."

Carlos glowered. "Tony, I'm trying to solve a problem here, but all I'm getting from you is a bunch of excuses."

Mary almost jumped out of her chair. "Tony, I'd swear you've been talking to Marvin or Pat! This is exactly the kind of conversation we have. When I ask them what's holding them back, they come out with all these lame excuses, blaming the economy, our prices, unfair competition — anything and anybody who's not in the room."

Lloyd said, "Sounds like my daughter, too. Whenever my wife or I talk to her about her grades or her room or any other problem, she gives us one excuse after another."

"Okay, Lloyd," said Tony. "This time I'll be Tony, a student whose grades are not so great. And Mary will play my mother. That way, Lloyd, you can sit back and be a neutral observer. Okay?"

"Great," said Lloyd. "That would be nice, for a change."

"Mary, you've just asked me to sit down and talk about my latest report card."

"All right," said Mary. "Tony, we've talked about your grades before, and here we are again, looking at one D-minus, four D's, and one C-minus. What do you have to say for yourself?"

"Well, you know," said Tony, looking at the floor, "some of those courses are real tough."

"Tony, I know you're much smarter than your grades show, so why aren't we seeing grades that are as good as you are smart?"

"Because Mrs. Jones doesn't like me. That's why. She didn't like me last year in biology and she doesn't like me this year in chemistry."

"Well, even if that were true, it doesn't explain all the other poor grades. But let's stick with Mrs. Jones for a minute. What makes you think she doesn't like you?"

Lloyd interrupted. "Hey, I've been down this trail before. It gets worse. Tony will explain why Mrs. Jones doesn't like him, and then Mary will argue with him about that, and pretty soon you find yourself sloshing around in the Swamp of No Escape."

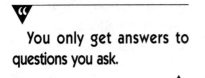

You only get answers to questions you ask.

Mary nodded vigorously. "I could feel myself sliding. I was getting sucked in. And I didn't know how to turn it around."

Tony smiled. "What you just experienced is a very common pattern for this kind of interrogation. Here's a question: would it be fair to say that you only get answers to questions you ask?"

There was a pause while they thought about it. Then all five nodded in agreement.

"Good. If you're taking notes, that's a good thing to write down.

"Now I'm going to give you five steps — note-takers, take note — for discussing performance problems that will not only keep you from getting pulled into this pattern — this, uh — what did you call it, Lloyd? Swamp of No Exit?"

"No Escape."

"Sounds vicious. Well, you'll do more than just avoid that. You'll be able to discuss performance issues in a way that elicits commitment, rather than just excuses or grudging compliance.

"A large part of avoiding the swamp is asking the right questions. Ask the wrong question, and you'll get the wrong answer — one that doesn't give you the information you need." Tony wrote on the board:

## 1. DEFINE THE ISSUE

"First step: Before you ask the first question, state the performance issue. Make it a plain statement of fact. Don't make judgmental statements, don't blame anybody, and don't jump to evaluating the problem. Statements like these are often seen as a personal attack, and so they get a defensive response or a counterattack, and nobody wins these battles. But if all you're doing is defining the performance issue factually, it's almost like informational feedback. It's not positive. It's not negative. It just is.

"This is very important: describe the behavior in performance terms rather than evaluative or judgmental terms. Think of your statement as a mirror. If the facts you state are clear and indisputable, not loaded with opinion or blame, the person will see an exact image of his own behavior. Then he can begin to change that behavior.

"The individual should understand that you are not attacking him but simply describing a behavior or performance problem that needs to be addressed and solved. The underlying message should be 'I like and respect you, but not your behavior.'

"In each of your situations, here's how you might provide factual descriptions of performance:

"Mike, your statement might be 'George, I've noticed that your math test scores are all between 70 and 80.'

"Janet, for you it might be 'I've begun to realize that all of us — myself included — sometimes get so busy with 'stuff' that we forget to do the teamwork kind of things that make such a big difference in how we function as a unit.'

"Carlos, for you a factual description to a plant manager could be 'I've looked at the plant productivity reports, and I see you're tracking between 97.2 and 98.1 percent.'

"For you, Lloyd, a factual description of grades might be something like 'Lori, I see you have a C, three D's, and a D-minus on this semester's report card."

"And yours, Mary, could be 'Marvin — or Pat — I've noticed that over the last six months your sales performance has sometimes slipped below 80.'

"That's all your opening statement should be. If you simply state the facts and don't say anything that sounds like you're assigning blame or you've already made up your mind, you avoid putting the individual on the defensive. This makes it easier to get to the heart of the problem."

Next, Tony wrote:

## 2. ASK FOR SOLUTIONS

"Now, here's the second step. Follow up with a future-oriented, neutral question. This is where most of you got into trouble. Remember what we said about questions? 'You only get answers to questions you ask.'

"Both Carlos and Mary started out with a statement of fact, although Mary front-loaded hers with something that sounded like an accusation: 'We've talked about your grades before, and here we are again.' Mary, this approach is more likely to hamper open communication than help it. Do you see that?"

"Yes, Tony, now that I've heard you repeat it, I can understand why it sounds like I've already assigned blame. I guess I'm just tired of worrying about your terrible grades." The others laughed.

"Well, I'll try to do better. Now, the next thing you and Carlos did, both of you, was to ask questions that looked backward rather than forward. Mary, you asked two in a row: 'What do you have to say for yourself?'

and 'Why aren't we seeing grades that are as good as you are smart?' Carlos, your first question, a two-for-one, was 'What's going on? Why are we suddenly turning out more defective units?' You also used the loaded word 'why,' rather than 'what' or 'how,' which have less emotional charge.

"The best approach is to avoid questions that are historical in nature, that can be answered yes or no, and that begin with 'why' or 'who.' Historical questions go back in time — 'Why did this go wrong?' 'Who caused the problem?' They ask for reasons, but they invite excuses. We don't like excuses, so we get upset when others offer them. But the fault is ours as much as theirs. All they're doing is trying to answer the question we asked: 'Why did this happen?' If instead we ask future-oriented questions, such as 'How can this be corrected?' or 'What can we do to reverse this trend?' we invite positive statements about how something could be done better in the future.

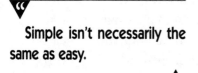

**Simple isn't necessarily the same as easy.**

"Here's where it gets interesting. If the individual can articulate how a problem can be corrected or a behavior improved, he's already done the brainwork necessary to determine what went wrong in the first place, and usually he'll explain that at the same time he's offering his solution. Once that's happened, there's no reason to demand an admission of guilt."

"That seems simple enough," said Mary.

"It is simple," said Tony. "But simple isn't necessarily the same as easy. When you see it in action, it's simple to understand. But changing old habits is not easy, as you'll see the first few times you try this approach."

"Tony," said Carlos, "what if you're asking for solutions but getting off-the-wall answers? Ideas that are totally impractical or unrealistic?"

"Well, that leads right into step three," said Tony:

## 3. EXPLORE OPTIONS

"Think of your dialogue as a brainstorming session. Don't evaluate each solution as it comes up; this is not the right time. Allow any suggestion the individual wants to make. Don't stop as soon as you hear the answer you want to hear. Just keep inviting solutions, staying as close to your original words as you can.

"This is usually the hardest step. Your tendency is to jump in and explain why a particular idea won't work. The wackier the idea, the more tempted you are to shoot it down in flames. I'll demonstrate.

"The sales manager asks, 'How can we increase sales on a unit volume basis?'

"Sales rep says, 'Drop the price by 20 percent.'

"Sales manager: 'Okay, one possibility is to reduce the price. How else might we be able to increase sales volume?'

"Sales rep: 'Well, I guess we could . . . '

"Now, as sales manager, you know a 20 percent price cut is not an option, but you want to keep the ideas flowing. If you keep asking for options and alternatives, you stand a good chance of getting your sales rep back on the track of solving his own problem. The less you talk, the more suggestions he will make, and the more he'll feel he owns the solution. Besides, he probably knows more than you do about how to get things moving again.

"Once the ideas are laid out, you can ask another question, along the lines of 'Which of these ideas could we realistically implement to start getting sales back where they ought to be?'

"Which brings us to step four.

## 4. REINFORCE POSITIVE RESPONSES

"Reinforce any useful suggestions he makes. Once you've finished compiling suggestions and started reviewing them one by one, focus positive attention on the best ones. Let's say the sales rep suggests trying a new point-of-purchase advertising approach because the current materials seem to get bent out of shape easily. You can say, 'Marvin, that's an excellent suggestion. This is the kind of thinking that will get our sales back on track.' What you're doing is encouraging him to keep coming up with new ideas — and he will, as long as you keep giving him positive reinforcement. You're also keeping the discussion going, giving him more opportunities."

"What if Marvin just keeps coming up with excuses?" asked Mary.

"Okay, why don't you role play that with me? You be Marvin, and I'll be you. Whenever I ask you something, give me an excuse."

"No problem, Tony. I've heard 'em all. Even invented a few myself when I was a sales rep." Everyone laughed.

"Okay, Marvin," said Tony, "how can we get sales back up where they should be?"

"Well, I don't know. Sales are down everywhere."

"I see that. How could we overcome that trend here at Caribou Creek?"

"I really don't know. The economy is pretty tight."

"Yes, it is tight. What can we do to get a bigger slice of the market?"

Mary smiled. "That's pretty good. You just keep coming back with 'what' or 'how' questions no matter what he says, right?"

"Exactly. Keep asking questions that steer the discussion toward future goals. Don't let him sidetrack you with what's happened in the past."

"Does that work with kids?" asked Lloyd.

"Sure," said Tony. "You be a student and I'll be the parent. Okay, Lloyd, how can we get your grades up to C's or better?"

"I don't know. All the courses I'm taking now are pretty tough."

"I'm sure they are tough. Still, I'm curious. What can we do to get to the point where all of your grades are C or above?"

"I don't know."

"Well," said Tony, "if you did know, what would your answer be?"

Lloyd, surprised, stammered, "Well, I — I guess I could study some more. . . . Hey, that's a pretty tricky question, Tony!"

"I don't know if it's tricky," said Tony, "but it does work. You can't use it all the time, but in the right circumstances it helps the person realize he does know, after all. You have to keep in mind, especially with kids, that 'I don't know' is sometimes just another way of saying 'I don't want to think about it.'"

Janet frowned. "Tony, what if you ask him, 'If you did know, what would your answer be?' and he still doesn't know?"

"You could just say, 'Well, think about it for a while and I'll check with you again tomorrow or next week' or whatever is appropriate. Then you ask your first question again. In any case, it's important to reinforce any useful ideas the individual comes up with. If there are limits you have to work within, disclose them up front. Say, 'Within the confines of our quarterly budget, how can we get sales back where they should be?' or 'Given that you are involved in basketball and track, how can we get your grades up to C's or better?'

"Okay, is this part clear? Any questions? No? Then on toward the finish line. The final step is —

## 5. CLOSE THE DEAL

"— wrap everything up. What you're really doing here is getting the individual's commitment to accomplish a certain task or achieve certain results. Basically, you should summarize your discussion and propose an agreement. Something like this: 'Pat, I think we've agreed that we don't have the market penetration we would like in Oregon, and that to bring your gross margin up to a good, solid 22, your best approach would be to target five or six high-potential accounts and upgrade our point-of-purchase advertising.'

"For a child in school, you might say, 'Lori, I think what we've talked about and agreed on here is that if you study an hour or two every school night, rather than trying to jam it all into one day, your grades will get up to where they should be.' Or you might say, 'Lori, I think I know what we ended up agreeing on. What do you see as our agreement?'"

"What if I don't think an hour or two is enough to get the job done?" asked Lloyd.

"In this situation, I wouldn't be too concerned. There are probably a lot of factors holding her grades down, but if you have Lori's commitment to improve some of her study habits, she may make other helpful changes as well. And maybe you're wrong — maybe one or two hours *is* enough. On the other hand, if I were talking with a sales rep I'd probably want to be more specific.

"During the wrap-up, include positive expectations about the individual's ability to improve, as in 'Well, Pat, I think I agree with you that the new point-of-purchase materials and targeting those high-potential accounts will get your average back in the 22-point range. You're one of our most capable sales reps, and you have the skills to do this.'

"Finally, as part of the agreement, arrange a time to meet again. Lloyd, you might say to your daughter, 'Lori, let's check with each other again in two weeks and see how it's working. And if you need any help before then, please let me know.'

"Now let's take one final break before we wrap up today's session and send you out on your projects.

"And, as promised, here are the jokes. Enjoy. And I'd like tickets to your next stand-up gigs."

# Putting It to Work

## *What to Do Next*

"**S**o, folks," said Tony, "that's the whole thing in a nutshell. An all-day nutshell." They chuckled. "And now that you've learned everything there is to know about bringing out the best in others, the next thing you'll do is to go forth and put it into practice.

"Each of you will take the tools and techniques you've learned and apply them to your situation. For you, Janet, this means better teamwork. For Lloyd, better grades from Lori, and a cleaner room. For Carlos, it's plant productivity. For Mary, it's Marvin's and Pat's sales performance. And Mike will be aiming at better classroom performance from his students.

"Three of you have situations involving many people, while two of you are concerned with one or two individuals. This should be an interesting test of the principles in action. Some of you may decide to use all of the tools we've talked about. Others may find that you need only one or two of them. Some of you may already be using some or even all of the tools, but perhaps not as effectively as you could. Whatever you decide, I would like for you to put at least one of the tools to use within a week of leaving here. This is important, because you'll find that ninety days goes by pretty fast.

"In the few minutes we've got left, I'm going to give you some guidelines for applying these tools. Then I'll turn you loose. In ninety days I'll ask you all to meet here again. We'll tell one another how well it worked, or if it didn't work.

"We've talked about all the tools you'll need to bring out the best in the people you're dealing with. But the real learning is going to happen over the next three months. Unless you're different from all the other groups I've worked with, you'll stub your toe at least once. And every stubbed toe will be a learning situation that will strengthen your skills.

"Now, before I sum everything up for you in twenty-five words or less, do you have any other questions? Anything I haven't covered adequately?"

"Let me see if I understand this correctly," said Carlos, consulting his notes. "I go back and I communicate positive expectations about productivity. I make sure that people are accountable and establish some high-low targets. I provide graphs for the metrics I'd like to keep track of. I reinforce the good things I see people do, and when I confront substandard performance, I use future-oriented questions. And if I do these things, productivity will go up. Is that right?"

"You summed it up pretty well, Carlos. Yes, that's basically what we're saying. And if Janet uses the same principles — not necessarily the exact same actions, of course, and probably with a different style — the nursing staff's teamwork will improve. And so forth."

"Well," said Carlos somberly, "it sounds entirely too easy. Manufacturing is a very complex operation, and it takes lots of different kinds of people to run it. I hate to keep playing the role of the class skeptic, but in my experience, nothing that sounds simple turns out to be simple when you put it in practice."

"That's been my experience, too," said Tony. "It's never as easy as it sounds. Remember what I said a few minutes ago? Simple isn't the same as easy? That's what we're up against here. Because it isn't as simple as just getting the other person to change his behavior. That's the easy part.

> **The hard part is changing your own behavior.**

"The hard part is changing your own behavior.

"You have to look at the behavior of others, behaviors that you wish to modify. Then you have to examine your own behavior and ask yourself, 'What do I have to do — what changes do I have to make in my own behavior — in order to get others to do their best?' And you have to make those changes in a way that brings out the best in others."

"So what you're saying," said Lloyd, "is that it's more about changing my own behavior than changing the behavior of my daughter?"

"Absolutely!" said Tony. "It is absolutely about changing your own behavior. If you want Lori to change her behavior, you have to change your own behavior first.

"I don't want that to sound like I'm laying the blame for your daughter's poor grades on you, Lloyd, or your workers' performance on you, Carlos. That's not my intention at all. The point is this. Problems arise for a multitude of reasons, most of which are not necessarily any one person's fault. But once they arise, they get locked into our relationships and take on a life of their own. In trying to deal with them, we get into patterns that lead us around in circles. Remember the role playing we just finished doing? We ask, "Why did this happen?" and somebody answers with an excuse. Then we fall into the trap of arguing with the excuse. This leads us right back into the past, when what we really need is to break out of the cycle by looking toward the future.

"This is the part you will find hardest when you go back to your situations. You can't quite see this now, but when you really start thinking about these ideas and trying to put them into practice, you'll find yourself constantly fighting your own habits.

"The key is understanding that *you* have to change before you can expect others to change. Keep thinking about that when you start running into difficulty or setbacks. And you *will* hit setbacks. It's almost guaranteed."

"Tony," said Mary, "what if the problem is not so much behavior as attitude? If somebody wants to change, wants to bring in more sales, then I can see how he might respond to your expectations and feedback. But what if it's just a bad attitude?"

"Good question. Let's reframe it a bit. Instead of behavior versus attitude, let's look at it in terms of behavior versus nonbehavior. Attitude is nonbehavior, right?"

"Okay, if you want to define it that way, I guess so. But take Marvin, for example. I'm not sure whether Marvin's problem is basically a behavior problem or an attitude problem."

"What do you see that makes you think that there might be an attitude problem?" asked Tony.

"Well, when he gets into these slumps, he turns in reports late, and he doesn't take the trouble to target his best accounts. He stops planning his sales calls. He's totally unmotivated — just seems to shrug it off, as if he doesn't care. That's what I mean by 'attitude.'"

"Yes, I see what you mean. Well, it's tough to deal with generalities like 'attitude' or 'motivated.' If you tell Marvin that he needs to be 'more aggressive,' this doesn't tell him anything very useful. He may not have a clue how to go about being more aggressive. Your feedback, unfocused as it is, may encourage him to work harder, but he may waste energy on something that's irrelevant to what you want.

"But let me ask you this. If Marvin turned in his sales reports on time and wrote out a carefully thought out sales plan for each of his key accounts, would you conclude that his attitude was better?"

"Yes, I think so."

"But reporting and planning are behaviors, aren't they? And if these behaviors were improved, you would consider his attitude improved as well."

"Okay, so I need to identify specific behaviors I want Marvin to improve, and then reinforce — oh, I see where you're going! I need to change my behavior by making it a habit to reinforce him positively every time his behavior shows improvement. Instead of ignoring him, like I do now. Then his attitude — or what I'm calling his attitude but is actually his behavior — will improve."

"Now you've got it," said Tony.

"Let me see if I understand," said Mike. "Things like friendly, courteous, cheerful, pleasant, and neat are nonbehaviors, while saying thank you, listening politely, smiling, and turning in book reports on time are behaviors. Right?"

"Essentially," said Tony.

"And because we can't actually see the thing we call attitude or self-esteem, we draw conclusions based on the behavior we observe. So if we change the behaviors associated with 'self-esteem' or 'motivation,' then we make progress. That makes a lot of sense, and if I can keep that in mind, I don't think I'll have too much trouble using it."

"It's the same whether you're a teacher or a boss or a supervisor or a parent," said Tony. "Although we might be concerned with attributes or attitudes such as motivation or self-esteem, the only thing we can really affect

is behavior — getting to work on time, making cold calls, paying attention in class, or making beds. And modifying our own behavior is the key to changing the behavior of others — which in turn is the key to improved attitude, improved motivation, improved self-esteem.

"To carry it one step further, if you can produce the behaviors you want, they will lead to the results you want — higher production volume, better productivity, more sales, improved self-esteem, better grades, lower labor costs, faster cycle times, higher revenues, maybe even shorter hospital stays.

"From the point of view of metrics and feedback, it's best when you can show a direct connection between behavior and results, like studying and grades, or cold calls and sales. But in some cases you have to assume a relationship, because it's too expensive or takes too much time to measure. Janet, you may be confident that certain teamwork behaviors will lead to better patient care and lower costs, but actually showing the linkage might be difficult.

"Any other questions? Yes, Carlos."

"I guess I'm the designated hard-nose in this room, but I have to ask: What happens when you just have to chew someone out? It happens, you know."

"I'll grant that," said Tony. "But you need to keep certain things in mind. First, as often as not, we chew people out because we're angry or frustrated and it makes

*us* feel better. Probably doesn't help change their behavior — at least in the long run — but we do feel better. So if that's the case, at least acknowledge it.

> "Second, it's often the first action we take — but it should be the last. There are lots better ways to get lasting behavior change.

> **As often as not, we chew people out because we're angry or frustrated and it makes us feel better.**

> "Third, although it stops the wrong behavior — temporarily, at least — it doesn't necessarily get the right behavior to occur. You get the right behavior when you reinforce the right behavior.

"Fourth: as often as not, chewing out a person carries with it an implicit or explicit threat — 'If you don't get good grades, you're grounded for three weeks' — but we don't always follow through on the threat. If you're not prepared to pull the trigger, don't point the gun.

"Fifth, the principle of immediacy applies here the same as with positive reinforcement. If you do chew someone out, do it very, very, soon after the behavior.

"The most effective chewing out I ever got was in the army. I was a brand-new lieutenant going through branch training for the adjutant general corps. The class advisor was an infantry major with two tours of duty in combat. He'd made the 5 percent list to major, promoted ahead of his contemporaries. He was an airborne ranger. A chestful of combat decorations. Bronze medal in the decathlon in the Olympics. Tough. Straight shooter. I'm

sure there were many places he'd rather have been than with a bunch of noninfantry lieutenants.

"Anyway, I flunked an exam. Flat-out flunked it. He called me into his office. I was expecting to get reamed. Yelled at and all.

"I walked in and saluted. He looked up at me and never took his eyes off me. He never blinked. He never raised his voice.

"'Lieutenant Russo, you flunked this exam. What do you have to say for yourself?'

"'No excuse, sir,' I replied.

"'Do you think this will happen again?'

"'No sir!'

"'I didn't think so. Dismissed.'

"I have never, before or since, been so thoroughly chewed out. It was complete. But it wasn't the typical chewing out. So, sure, if you have to chew somebody out, do it. But do it sparingly. And do it effectively.

"Then be sure to reinforce the right behavior as soon as it occurs. Too often, someone gets chewed out and there's a little burst of improvement, but it doesn't get reinforced. So he slides back. Then he gets chewed out again. Little burst of improvement. No reinforcement. If this happens too many times, he'll just give up.

"Here's a good rule of thumb: Keep a positive-to-negative feedback ratio of three-to-one, four-to-one, or five-to-one. That is, try to give positive feedback three, four, or five times for every time you give negative feedback.

"Any more questions. No? Okay, here are the steps I want you to take in tackling your situation." Tony picked up the chalk and wrote on the last clean square of the chalkboard:

## 1. BEHAVIORAL CHANGE

"First step: decide what you want the individual to do, do differently, or stop doing. Do you want her to study more, study less, study differently, study different subjects, study in a different location, or something else? Mary, the results you're looking for from Marvin are improved sales levels. What kind of behaviors could he engage in that would lead to improved sales?

## 2. PERFORMANCE LEVEL

"Second, decide what a reasonable level of performance would be. Lloyd, what should Lori's grades look like? All A's, all C's, one D and the rest C's? Janet, how much teamwork would be appropriate? What would that look like? Carlos, how about plant productivity? Should it be 97 percent of potential, or 98.5 percent? You might want to think both short-term and long-term here. Remember the gradient stress scale. In ninety days, you may not be where you want to end up, but you should have made some progress.

## 3. YOUR BEHAVIOR

### a. Expectations

### b. Accountability

### c. Feedback

"Finally, examine your own behavior. There are, as we saw, three basic areas to consider. First, are there ways you can better communicate positive expectations? Not just your words, but your tone of voice and your body language. Pay attention to the setting, too. Don't allow interruptions by other people or calls. Let the person know the discussion is important to you.

"Second, examine the issue of accountability. Can you do a better job of helping the person focus on specific behaviors that lead to improved results? Is the person committed to specific goals? Is his accountability clear-cut? Are you using high-low targets to improve motivation?

"Third, feedback. Are you providing motivational feedback by reinforcing improvements in behaviors and results? Is it specific? Is it frequent enough? Is the person getting negative feedback for doing the right thing, or positive reinforcement for doing the wrong thing? How could you improve your own behavior to provide better reinforcement? Consider enlisting the support of others — colleagues, neighbors, your spouse — to help reinforce behavior.

"Are you offering informational feedback frequently enough and in sufficient detail and quantity to enable the person to improve his performance? Do you present it in an easy-to-understand graphic form? Is the person allowed to record data and maintain the graph himself?

"Finally, does the person's performance call for developmental feedback in the form of supportive confrontation of nonperformance? If this is appropriate, decide in advance what you're going to say and what questions you're going to ask. Avoid recriminations. Don't get bogged down in the past; emphasize future improvements in behavior and results.

"And that's it. Now I'm going to send you out into the world to do good deeds. Like the Five Musketeers.

"Remember, when we meet here again — check your schedules — I'm going to ask each of you to tell the rest of us what you did and how it worked. Between now and then, if you have any questions, feel free to give me a call."

# Mary's Sales Story

## *Win One, Lose One*

"Welcome back, Musketeers!" said Tony to the group of five. "It's been three months since our first meeting, and I assume they've been busy and productive months.

"I've been looking forward to hearing your stories. I always like to hear about the successes, of course, but there are usually a few instances where results are, shall we say, less than expected, and these are always intriguing. They make us think, and they end up teaching us new ways to approach a problem.

"So — let's start by hearing from our sales manager. If you remember, Mary had two sales reps that were not living up to their full potential — Marvin and Pat. Sometimes they would do well, but often they were in a slump. Mary, were you able to turn Marvin and Pat into full-time powerhouse reps?"

"Well, Tony," said Mary, "Let me keep you in suspense a little while longer. First I'd like to tell you what I did after I left here three months ago. I'll start from the beginning.

"After I got home, I reviewed my notes and thought about everything we had discussed. I was particularly struck by your reaction, Lloyd, when Tony asked you what you did when Lori occasionally brought home a higher grade. I remembered that the two of you had talked about 'extinction,' and when I saw that word again in my notes, I became more and more certain that's what I'd been doing with Marvin and Pat.

> **The only times I ever really talked with either of them was when they were in one of their periodic slumps.**

"The only times I ever really talked with either of them was when they were in one of their periodic slumps. Whenever performance improved, I said nothing. Not even a 'Nice job this month, Marvin,' or 'Way to go, Pat.'

"I began to realize that, like most people, they'd probably rather have negative feedback than no feedback at all, as if they didn't exist. So what I was doing was, in a peculiar way, reinforcing substandard performance and punishing or extinguishing good performance.

"You probably remember something I said at the

beginning of our first session — that I was unsure why Carlos, Janet, and I were in the same group as Mike and Lloyd, whose concerns were with children and their grades. Of course, I soon learned what we had in common, which was the need to motivate people to do their best, no matter what the job or task. And I began to understand this even more strongly when I thought about how I had been interacting with Marvin and Pat.

> **I soon learned what we had in common, which was the need to motivate people to do their best, no matter what the task.**

"Anyway, since both of them happened to be in a sales slump at the time of our first session, I didn't have anything to reinforce when I got back to work. So I decided the best way to get things moving was with developmental feedback — 'supportive confrontation of nonperformance,' I think you called it, Tony.

"I went back and carefully studied my notes on developmental feedback. I decided I needed to carefully plan everything I wanted to say during the first few minutes of the discussion I would have with each of them. I wrote down how I wanted to describe the performance issue. I designed the questions I needed to ask — several future-oriented 'what' and 'how' questions. I also wrote down how each might respond, as well as how I would react to the responses. I wanted nothing left to chance, as you can see." The others chuckled knowingly.

"It's kind of ironic, actually. I've always been very

detail-oriented, and I wouldn't think much of a sales rep who would go into a sales call without having spent some time planning it, knowing the customer's needs and the best way to approach him and so forth. But now I realized I wasn't preparing myself for my coaching sessions with all my sales reps. I was just winging it.

"I decided that, in my leadership role as a professional coach for my reps, I needed to prepare for every session, especially a developmental discussion. That's what I did.

"The next thing I did was to enlist the aid of my husband. I asked him to play the role of Marvin. We started playing out our scene. It turned out to be a real eye-opener. Although I had written down the questions I wanted to ask, I wanted to make it as realistic as possible, so I did it without looking at my notes.

"For the first couple of minutes I did okay. Then, all of a sudden, I heard myself asking, 'But *why* did your sales drop off?'

"I couldn't believe it. As soon as the words came out of my mouth, I knew it was the wrong kind of question. But, out of habit, I had asked it anyway.

"We started again. Would you believe it? About three or four minutes into our little scene, I found myself asking 'why' questions again. It was frustrating. I knew the kinds of questions I needed to ask, but I still kept slipping back into my old habits.

"My husband found this amusing, which made me even madder. So I suggested we switch roles so I could see what it felt like from Marvin's point of view. I also secretly wanted to see him get tripped up on the same questions, of course. When you've been married fourteen years you take your revenge in subtle ways." Janet and Carlos laughed out loud at this. Lloyd smiled and continued writing on his note pad.

Mary continued: "Well, I was right. Much to his surprise, my husband found himself asking 'why' questions just as I had. And naturally I took great joy in pointing this out to him. As it turned out, though, I learned more from playing Marvin than from playing myself. When my husband kept asking questions like 'Why did you lose that sale?' I found myself growing more and more irritated. I felt like I was being attacked. I would answer by describing in great detail all the reasons I could think of for why I had failed to close this sale or meet that quota. That taught me the difference between being asked 'Why did this failure occur?' and 'What can we do to get back to 110 percent of quota?'"

Lloyd said, "Probably the same as the difference between 'Why are there still D's and F's on your report card?' and 'What can we do to get everything up to at least a C?'"

"Exactly," said Tony.

Mary continued, "We spent most of the afternoon role playing the 'Mary and Marvin Show.' Then I spent another hour or so tweaking what I wanted to say and memorizing it. That sounds like a long time, but I was

determined to get my part right. I realized how important it was — not just for getting Marvin back on his
game, but for use with all my other reps. I think sometimes we get so busy we
forget that coaching is really
the core of our job. A few
hours spent learning how to
be a better sales coach could
mean a lot of sales and many
thousands in extra revenue.

> **A few hours spent learning how to be a better sales coach could mean a lot of sales and extra revenue.**

"The next morning, I asked Marvin to come to my
office for our usual status meeting, in which we discuss
current sales figures and the trends we expect over the
next few months. We chatted about this and that for a
couple of minutes. Then I said, 'Marvin, I've been looking at your sales performance over the last twelve months,
and I see that you've ranged between 80 and 120 percent of target. Now, I've seen you when you're at the top
of your form, and there are few people who can match
you. When you're on, you're one of our top performers.
I know your capabilities, and so do you. I'm wondering
what we can do to get you consistently into the range of
110 to 120 percent.'"

"Is that exactly the way you said it?" asked Tony.

"Yes, I'm sure of it. I practiced it over and over until
I had it down pat, and until I could sound natural. I felt
it was important to get off on the right foot.

"I knew Marvin didn't look forward to these 'heart-to-hearts,' and sure enough, his first reaction was to avoid answering my 'how could we' questions. When I asked him how we could get sales back to 120, he said, 'That's tough. The markets are tight right now.'

"So I said, 'Yes, I know the market has been tough. So how can we get around that and back up to 120?'

"He said, 'The competition is really fierce.'

"We went back and forth like this a few times, and he kept halfheartedly giving me these generalized excuses. I was beginning to worry that my approach was all wrong. But because I was consciously trying to modify my own behavior and was paying close attention to his responses, I gradually became aware of an interesting thing that was happening.

"Usually in these talks, Marvin and I would start to get a little hostile toward each other, then we'd both back off, and we'd never get around to specific issues. When the meeting was over, he'd leave in a bit of a huff, and his sales would pick up for a while, and then the cycle would start all over again.

"This time, though, I felt that I was staying calm and objective, focusing mostly on the discussion of where we could go in the future, and very little — only when I dropped back into my old ways — on criticizing Marvin for the past. He'd waffle and dodge, but I just stayed cool and brought the subject back to ways we might overcome the difficulties.

"Finally, feeling a little frustrated, I said, 'Marvin, I know it's tough out there, and I know the competition is fierce, but I also know you can get to 120 and stay there because you know your products and you know your accounts. So I'm asking you, because you're my expert in these things, what can we do to get from here to there?'

"Well, all of a sudden, the dam just broke. He started giving me a stream of ideas. Some were a little iffy, but others were much stronger and full of potential. I could tell he was a little angry and frustrated that I just kept asking the same question over and over. But I sensed that he was angry at himself as much as at me. Once he started reeling out the ideas, they just kept coming.

"In the end, he promised me two things. First, he would target Caribou Creek Gold. That's our premium product, the one with the highest margins. He promised me a 12 percent increase in Gold volume without losing more than 6 percent of sales in other products in that particular line. That seemed reasonable, because even if the others dropped a full 12 percent, our overall sales revenue would go up, along with our gross margin. He also agreed to target ten high-potential accounts and increase volume in five of those by 10 percent within ninety days. We ran the numbers and figured that, sure enough, meeting these goals would put him somewhere between 100 and 120 percent.

"Since that first meeting, we've met and talked for a few minutes each Friday about his activities and progress. And guess what? Sales on Caribou Creek Gold are up — are you ready for this? Not 12 percent. Not 24 percent. They're up 87 percent! And the sales on other products have not dropped — in fact, they've gone up almost 1 percent! I wouldn't have predicted this at all. But it's true. True, true, true.

"Bottom line: I did that coaching session in my first week back. Marvin was at 81 percent. Four weeks later, overall sales were up 17 percentage points. And they've continued to climb. Right now, they're running about 115 percent and still climbing."

"That's terrific!" exclaimed Tony. "You did a lot of good work. Now what about Pat?"

"Ah, yes. Pat. Obviously, he was part of the rehearsal I did with my husband. And I planned everything just as I did with Marvin. The first part of the conversation actually seemed to go better than it did with Marvin. He made promises, and we had meetings, and I reinforced him, just like with Marvin.

"And what happened? Nothing. Nada. Rien. Pat's sales just sort of meandered up and down like they did before. I was raised in Texas, and when someone talked a good game, but that was it, we used to say, 'This guy is all hat and no cattle.' Well, Pat was all hat and no cattle."

"And?"

"Five weeks ago, I gave him thirty days to improve his performance to 95 percent and keep it there or above."

"And?"

"He got it to 90 percent within two weeks. And then it dropped again."

"Where is it now?"

"It isn't anywhere. He doesn't work for me anymore. I fired him three days ago. In retrospect, I didn't step up to the situation soon enough — not with Marvin, and certainly not with Pat. Half the battle for me was just stepping up to the situation. The truth of the matter is that I didn't fire Pat. His performance fired him. I just carried the message.

> **In retrospect, I didn't step up to the situation soon enough.**

"The thing I like about this approach is that it gives me the confidence to step up to any future situation involving nonperformance. It's a good, solid, middle position between yelling and screaming on the one hand and being a wimp on the other. Works for me."

# Janet's Health Care Story

## *Building Teamwork*

"**W**ho's next?" asked Tony, looking around the room. "Janet?"

"I'm ready," said Janet. "My case, as you remember, is a bit different, because what I wanted to accomplish was more difficult to measure than what most of you were doing. Instead of numbers on a chart, like Mary's sales volume and dollars, I knew our feedback would have to be more subjective. I remembered our discussion of choosing a few key targets and recording how often the nurses and I agreed on whether we're accomplishing them. But it's still a 'soft' metric, compared to others.

"Tony, you also showed us that terms like 'highly motivated' or 'good teamwork' weren't of much use unless you could describe specifically what they meant. So I decided the first thing I had to do was list some things I considered good teamwork. I asked myself, 'Do

I know it when I see it?' The answer was yes. So I started writing down what teamwork looks like when I see it on the floor. I came up with a list of four specific kinds of behavior that I could monitor and reinforce.

> I asked myself, 'Do I know good teamwork when I see it?'

"My first measure of teamwork is how well new people are brought up to speed. Because of nursing shortages and turnover, we have to fill vacant positions constantly, and even then, we frequently have to hire temps to help out. Either way, it's important for these new people to feel comfortable as soon as possible in their jobs. What behaviors are important in getting this done? I can think of quite a few. First, we need to welcome them and thank them for coming. We show them where the supplies are and how to do the paperwork. We teach them our patient care protocols. Rather than dumping on them, we start them out on less complicated cases and easier duties until they're into the swing of things. And we also let them know that we are ready to help them any way we can and answer any and all questions.

"Second, a good sign of teamwork for me is to see two or more nurses working together on a task. That often makes it easier to get the job done, and it's an identifiable behavior, so it's easy to keep track of.

"Third was communication. I grouped several be-haviors under this heading. One of them is listening well, because every scrap of information is important when you're caring for patients, and listening to each other is part of good teamwork. But the flip side is that just listening isn't enough. You have to be able and willing to express yourself, because it isn't good teamwork when one or two people are always dominant and others never speak up.

"Communication was interesting for me because I found I had to change my own behavior. In the past, when I talked with groups of my nursing staff, I would see one or two of them whose body language should have told me they had something to say but were reluctant to speak. I would just charge ahead and go on to other topics. Now I realized I should draw them out, find out what they had to say, and get them more actively involved. I had to learn to say, 'Emily, I can see you might have some thoughts about this. I'd really like to hear them, because I think what you have to say might be very helpful.'

"I soon discovered that people learn quickly by example. After I had drawn a few nurses out this way, one of the senior nurses who tended to dominate the discussions started turning to the quieter team members and asking for their opinions. This was another marker of good teamwork, one that I hadn't anticipated. I was secretly pleased to see it happening, and I congratulated myself for being such a good role model.

"And then, a couple of days later, it suddenly hit me: I hadn't done a thing to reinforce this new behavior.

I was extinguishing it even as it was getting started! So I made it a point to tell my senior nurse how much I appreciated her bringing everybody into the discussion, and that this was sure to improve our teamwork.

"My fourth teamwork indicator, one that's also related to communication, is sharing information freely. All too often — and I know this happens in other organizations — people either consciously or unconsciously hoard information that is vital to good teamwork. So whenever I saw someone sharing information of any kind, I reinforced that behavior. Of course, there's a lot you can't share in a hospital, such as personal or private medical information, but I encouraged staff to share appropriate news about patients or staff members — for example, when Mary Jones, one of our housekeepers, recently lost her mother, and when the daughter of one of our patients was elected president of the student council.

"I put this list together about three or four days after I got back. I've been to a lot of seminars, and I always come back all fired up, but then I get caught up in my job again and keep putting things off. But I remembered what you said, Tony, about getting started the first week, so I forced myself to sit down one night and get something down on paper.

"Once I had my list in hand, the thing that really opened my eyes was how many opportunities I was

missing to reinforce people who were doing exactly what
I wanted them to do. Someone would do something,
and a minute or two later I'd go — " Janet slapped her
forehead — "'Well, duh, Janet, that's good teamwork,
and why don't you tell them
so?' Making up the list sen-
sitized me to these behaviors. Without it, I would
never have realized how
much good teamwork I was
extinguishing.

> **I was missing opportunities
> to reinforce people who were
> doing exactly what I wanted
> them to do.**

"I began to see other
opportunities I was missing.
I had started by looking at teamwork within the department, but there's also teamwork *between* departments,
and often that's even harder to come by.

"There was one department in particular that we
had been at loggerheads with, and that was OR. We
weren't exactly fighting with them, but there was definitely tension in the air. They can help us a lot by giving
us a heads-up on what they're doing with a patient —
that they're bringing him down at 3:15 instead of 3:30
or the patient will have an IV going or something. Well,
sometimes that heads-up would happen and sometimes
it wouldn't, and when it didn't, it often caused problems on our end.

"I started thinking about several recent incidents.
I replayed in my mind some of the discussions that had
ended with both sides getting huffy with each other —
and discovered that it happened mostly when I asked

'why' questions. Usually it went something like this: 'You know that it would really help us if you'd let us know in advance what you're going to do, so why is it that we can't ever seem to get a heads-up from you?' The truth of the matter is that they were actually doing a pretty good job — just not as good as they could. Of course, every time I asked a 'why' question, they'd come back with a 'because' answer, the same way Marvin and Pat would do with Mary.

"So at our next meeting, I made it a point to stick to 'what' and 'how' questions: 'What can we do so we can work together better on this?' 'How can we do our part better?' I was pleased to see that this went over very well — mainly, I think, because my choice of words recognized that we were all in this together. And, as it turned out, there *were* some areas where we weren't doing our part. We all left that meeting feeling a lot better about it.

"Then I decided to enlist some help from our ward clerk, Ben. He plays a pivotal role — orders the labs, gets the X-rays, makes sure the meds are administered. He coordinates with admissions, OR, ER, and everybody else. So I took Ben to lunch one day. I briefly explained the three principles of expectations, accountability, and feedback, and I asked him to do one thing for me over the next thirty days. I asked him to pay attention to things other departments were doing to help us, and to make it a point to reinforce them five or ten times a day.

"Of course, the two of us had to come up with a list of positive behaviors to watch for — things like calling ahead to tell us they were bringing a patient down.

"Ben had already been doing a pretty good job of reinforcing, and other departments had been good about helping us. But after our lunch, Ben started reinforcing more specifically. He'd say things like 'Thanks very much for calling. Even five or ten minutes' notice helps us out and lets us get set up better. We really appreciate it.' Now the other departments are even better about communicating with us. They act more like a part of our team.

"About two weeks ago, I started using some of these techniques on the doctors. Well, you know MDs — some of them think they *are* the team. They go into a room to do a procedure, and when they leave, it looks like a tornado came through, and the nurses have to clean it up. So when I saw a doc helping out by throwing stuff in the garbage instead of just dropping it, I told him how much the nurses and I appreciated that.

"Now, that's only one doc, and it's the only time in the last two weeks I've seen him in a situation where he could help out that way. And we all know that one time does not a change make. But I think it's working.

"I don't want to give the impression that all this was a piece of cake. The meeting with OR involved more gnashing of teeth than I care to go into. And if I had it to do over, I probably would have involved my team more in determining what constituted good teamwork. But the results are just as I've said. It's like Tony told us: the hard part is changing your own behavior.

"There was another thing that happened, in an area that wasn't even part of teamwork — at least not directly. Volunteers play a huge role in the delivery of health care. We have volunteers working in labs, running the book cart, working in our New Life Center — they're everywhere. And lest you think 'volunteering' means 'running around smiling at people,' these folks all go through screening, orientation, and training. They have job descriptions and a supervisor. Obviously, though, as volunteers they receive no economic reward.

"It struck me one day that, although I appreciated the heck out of these folks, I didn't express it enough. So when the book cart came through the next day, I walked up to the volunteer running it and told her how much I appreciated her contribution to the well-being of our patients, her commitment to their recovery, her involvement in the community, and a host of other ways she was contributing. I acknowledged her fully.

"She was so moved that tears came to her eyes. She smiled softly and said, 'Thank you very much. That means so much to me.'

"And ever since then, she gives me a quick smile whenever she comes through. I'm not sure that it's made any difference in anything she does, but she sure feels better for it, and so do I. Maybe teamwork is better for what I did and maybe it's not. But it was the right thing to do.

"I can tell you this. My department functions a lot better now. Things run more smoothly. We're pulling together as a team much, much better. Communication has improved, and we get more cooperation from other departments. I feel more effective as a leader. I feel like I'm making more of a difference and having a more positive effect on people's lives. I can't say that the improved teamwork has affected our patients' vital signs or that they're being discharged sooner, but I can tell you that, on the whole, they seem more cheerful and upbeat. And that means they'll get well faster.

"Although the area I picked wasn't easily quantifiable, it was fairly straightforward to work on. Now that I have the tools and techniques down, I'm going to tackle something else. I'm not sure what, but applying these three keys to my 'project' has sharpened my skills in this area, so now I'm looking for a new project.

"Besides, it's been good for me. About two weeks ago my husband said, 'You seem a lot happier with your work lately.' I told him he was right. He asked me why, and I said it was because of what I had learned in this program.

"'What's the name of that program again?' he asked. I told him, 'Bringing Out the Best in Others.'

"'Well,' he said, 'it seems to have brought out the best in you, too.'"

# Lloyd's Parenting Story

## *The Things That Count*

"So, Lloyd," said Tony, "did you and Lori come up with a plan to improve her grades and get her room picked up?"

"Great news! Both situations are resolved. And a lot more. The last ninety days turned out to be a period of reflection and introspection for me. But first, let me back up a bit.

"After our first session three months ago, Mike and I grabbed a bite to eat. I wanted a teacher's perspective, so I asked him which of the three factors — expectations, responsibility, or feedback — would help me most in working with Lori on her grades. He told me there was something even more fundamental that had to come first.

"He told me the most important thing a teacher — or parent — had to do was create a safe environment. 'In order to learn,' he said, 'children need to feel both physically and emotionally safe.'

"I asked him, 'What exactly do you mean, "emotionally safe"?'

"'Kids are very vulnerable emotionally, Lloyd,' he told me. 'Their biggest fear is looking foolish or stupid in front of everybody else. And teachers set the tone. If the teacher belittles or ridicules a student for getting something wrong, it's a public humiliation. The other students spend half their time teasing or pitying the poor kid, and the other half living in fear of being called on in class themselves. It makes for a really poisonous learning atmosphere.

"Then he said — correct me if I get this wrong, Mike — 'Feeling emotionally safe is understanding that it's okay to make mistakes.' He said that making mistakes is in fact a good thing, because it's the best way to learn. We try new things, we explore, and usually we stub our toes a few times. But when we make a mistake, we remember it sharply, and to avoid making it again, we go another direction. I especially like how you summed up, Mike, and I wrote this down afterward. You said, 'Mistakes guide us toward the truth.'

> **Feeling emotionally safe is understanding that it's okay to make mistakes.**

"He told me about a kindergarten teacher — why don't you tell it, Mike?"

"Sure," said Mike. "This is someone I used to work with at another school — Avis Murphy was her name. Kids came out of her kindergarten class as fearless learners.

She did away with the whole idea of mistakes — even discouraged the use of the word. She called them 'learning takes.' The kids loved it. Whenever someone goofed up, or plans didn't go as expected, or things didn't come out the way they were supposed to, they would say, 'Oops! Well, there goes another learning take.' Then they would talk about what they had learned from it. Nobody felt bad about making a 'learning take,' and nobody got razzed. Sometimes Avis would make a mistake, and the kids would say, 'Hey, what a great learning take, Ms. Murphy!'

"Children are naturally curious. They want to know everything. Ever hang around with preschoolers? It's 'What's that, Daddy?' and 'Why is this, Mommy?' all day long. When you create an environment where there's no such thing as a stupid question, and where mistakes are not bad things but part of learning, kids feel that the people around them care about them. They can feel this caring, this love, in what you say to them, as well as in the way you act around them, the way you greet them when they come into the classroom, the way you shake their hand or hug them when they need a hug. This is true both in school and at home. And their natural curiosity, their thirst for knowledge and experience, can blossom. Within safe boundaries, of course — you don't want your kid tying on a cape to see how Superman flies out of a third-story window."

"I agree with Mike," said Lloyd. "What a smart, dedicated teacher this Avis Murphy is. By telling me about her, Mike made me realize that children need to know and feel that you love them unconditionally, and that their mistakes don't make you love them less.

> "
> **Children need to know and feel that you love them unconditionally, that their mistakes don't make you love them less.** 》

"Mike's story also made me think about what kind of learning environment I was creating for Lori. I told myself I was doing everything possible to make it safe for her, both physically and emotionally. After all, wasn't I giving her a roof over her head? Wasn't I buying her clothes and food and books and music, all the things that are important to a child's intellectual development? Wasn't I showing my interest in her schoolwork?

"But there was this knot in the pit of my stomach. And over the next few days, that knot grew bigger and harder. I was already aware that I had been guilty of extinction by not positively reinforcing Lori's improvements, however few and slight. I began to think I had been too hard on her, too focused on the negatives. In spite of my good intentions, I probably wasn't doing much to help her.

"Surely she knew that I cared, that I loved her no matter what. Surely she felt safe and secure in every way. But when I tried to put myself in Lori's place and look at the situation through her eyes, I grew more and more aware that this wasn't necessarily true, that perhaps she didn't feel she was loved unconditionally.

"From her perspective, it must have seemed that my love was conditional. Yes, I was there, not saying much, more or less in the background, as she struggled with her schoolwork. But if she got a poor grade, that's when she got my attention. I was like a malevolent presence hovering in the shadows, ready to pounce on any mistake.

"Seeing myself this way wasn't very pretty. I was a demon on accountability but a no-show on motivational reinforcement. I was doing a pretty lousy job on developmental feedback, too. And although I knew she could do better, I guess my expectations had fallen pretty low, and she probably sensed that.

"I was becoming the Anti-Pygmalion — taking a promising young woman and turning her into a dull, sad chunk of stone.

"After a few days of confronting myself with this, I decided that the first thing I had to do was create the feel-safe environment that Mike had so eloquently illustrated. So I took the steps Tony described for — let me see if I can remember your six-dollar term, Tony — for 'supportive confrontation of nonperformance.'" Everybody chuckled, including Tony.

"But I decided to apply them to my own behavior. I would talk with Lori, but this time we wouldn't talk about her grades. We would talk about our relationship.

"When I told her I wanted to talk with her, she gave me one of those eye-rolling looks and flopped into a chair. I said to her, 'Honey, I know you think I want to gripe about your grades again. But not today. What I want today is for you to help me with something.' She just looked at me.

"I went on: 'I want you to know that I am committed to helping you get better grades. But what I want now is for you to tell me how well I am doing. Am I being supportive enough?'

"She shrugged and gave me a typical teen non-answer: 'Yeah, I guess.'

"I tried again. 'Is the way I'm talking to you about grades helping or hurting you?' I asked gently.

"'I dunno,' she said.

"We went back and forth like this a few times. Then I remembered what we learned about 'what' and 'how' questions, questions about the future. I asked her, 'What am I not doing to support you that I could be doing? How can I be more supportive?'

"Suddenly her voice broke and she started crying, and I felt terrible, because I knew then that she did not feel emotionally safe around me. She didn't feel I loved her unconditionally.

"I was never happy with her, she said. She lived in fear of bringing home her report card because she knew it would make me angry. She said that when one of her grades did get better, I didn't seem to notice, but if one dropped, I sure jumped all over her for that. She felt there was no way she could win.

"So I spent most of an hour trying to establish the beginnings of a safe environment for her. She yelled at me. She sobbed uncontrollably. She wept silently. She hugged me. I cried. I told her I was sorry. We had a real dialogue. We talked honestly and openly for the first time in her life.

"It was an emotional roller coaster, I have to admit. I told her I could see how it must have seemed to her that I only looked for reasons to criticize her, but that I was doing the best I could with my limited skills. I told her that I had learned a lot in the past few days and in the past few hours, and that I would try harder not to be so negative. I told her I wanted her to feel that she could ask for my help with any problem.

"Finally she said, 'Dad, do you really think I can get better grades?'

"I said, 'I'm sure of it, honey.'

"She said, 'You are? What kind of grades do you think I can get?'

"And I said, 'Well, what kind of grades do *you* think you should be getting?'

"She said, 'Well, there's only three weeks left in this period, but I think maybe I can get all C's this time.'

"I said, 'I'll bet you *can* do it. And if everything really comes together and you could get a B in one subject, which subject would that be?'

"She said, 'English.'

"I said, 'Great! And I want you to know that you can come to me for help at any time. I'll do the best I can to help you meet that goal.'

"For the next three weeks, I kept track of my feedback responses, and I actually managed to beat that five-to-one positive ratio. So I had at least succeeded in modifying my own behavior, like you said. I complimented her every time I saw her studying. I said positive things every time she brought in a good score on a test or paper. If a grade dropped, I didn't mention it at all. The second time that happened, she said, 'Hey, Dad, you didn't mention the 68 I got on my math test.' I told her I figured she knew what needed improvement or would ask me if she needed help with it. I think she was testing me, because she didn't mention her low grades after that — and neither did I.

"After three weeks, she brought me her report card. This time she had a big smile on her face. She had four C's and two B's! And she finished the semester the same way. She was really glowing. And I don't mind telling you, I felt pretty good about it myself. I think I learned more than she did from it.

"Now that she's bringing home better marks every week, she's gaining all kinds of confidence. I can see it in everything she does. She's happier, her mother's happier, and I'm happier.

"I called Mike and thanked him again for his insight and advice. Later, I got to thinking, 'You know, Mike really helped me get right with Lori, but there's probably another teacher or two involved here as well. Maybe I should call them up and thank them, too.

"So I started by calling Lori's English teacher. I told her I had noticed a lot of improvement in Lori's grades lately and wondered if she had also. She said she had indeed. I said that her work with Lori was obviously paying off, and I thanked her. She said, 'You know, we can do only so much here at school. You must be doing something right at home, too, because Lori is coming to class much more prepared and eager to learn. So I'd like to thank you, too.'

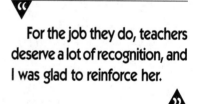

**For the job they do, teachers deserve a lot of recognition, and I was glad to reinforce her.**

"This teacher seemed surprised that I had called to thank her. My guess is she doesn't get many calls from grateful parents, and probably not enough positive feedback from students, colleagues, or the principal either. But for the job they do, teachers deserve a lot of recognition, and I was glad to reinforce her. I guess we were reinforcing each other.

"I felt so good telling her these things, and she seemed to appreciate it so much, that I immediately called all Lori's other teachers and did the same thing. Later I was telling my sister about this, and she said, 'I don't know if you remember, but the feedback ratio from Mom and Dad was probably one positive to a hundred nega-tive.' Which is probably true for most situations. We spend more time complaining about what's wrong than no-ticing what's right."

"So, Lloyd, that's great news about Lori's grades," said Tony. "Now what about the other issue, her room?"

Lloyd grinned. "Well, that's the most interesting part of this project. I don't know what she's done with it. I think it's probably messier than ever."

"You think?"

"Yeah. I haven't actually seen it for three weeks. Don't believe I want to, either." Mary and Janet laughed.

Mary leaned toward Janet and, in a stage whisper, said, "If it looks like my room did at that age, she's prob-ably an eighty-sixth-born." The whole room burst into laughter — Lloyd loudest of all.

After a moment, Lloyd continued: "Let me tell you what happened. About a month after we talked about her grades, I was feeling so virtuous about my new parenting skills that I decided to tackle the messy room issue. So I sat down with Lori and started asking her all the right kinds of questions.

"Her responses surprised me. She didn't get angry or defensive. She simply said, very calmly, 'I don't un-derstand why it's so important for my room to be neat. After all, it's not your room. It's *my* room.'

"I said, 'Yes, but your mother and I have to look at it because it's right at the top of the stairs.'

"She said, 'Then I'll just close my door. You say you don't like looking at what you consider a mess. That should solve the problem.'

"That stopped me in my tracks. She was right. It *was* her room.

"The only thing I could think to do at that point was call in my reinforcements — her mother. We negotiated some more. It couldn't become a fire hazard, we said. She agreed. Any clothes that got damaged by lying around on the floor would not be replaced by us. She agreed. If we could smell it with the door closed, she had to clean it. She agreed.

"It took a little getting used to, but it was the right thing to do. And I learned something new about Lori, something I really admire. When she's in the right, she's a good negotiator. Tough, but fair.

"So the fact is, I don't know what horrors lie beyond that door. When I pass by, I don't smell smoke — or anything else, for that matter — and I don't hear any loud noises, unless you count alternative rock and the occasional rap tune. I usually tap on the door and say, 'You okay in there?' and she says, 'Fine, Dad.'

"Tony, thanks to you — and you too, Mike — things are a lot better at home. We're all happier, and Lori feels safe and confident bringing problems to her mother and me and letting us know when she needs our help. And she knows that even if she isn't perfect in every way,

we still love her unconditionally. So — thanks, both of
you, from all three of us."

# Carlos's Productivity Story

## *Enhancing the Bottom Line*

"Lloyd, you're very welcome," said Tony. "I love to hear stories like yours. Makes my job especially worthwhile.

"Now, Carlos, can you top that?"

Carlos smiled. "Are you kidding? I'd have to go hug several hundred employees. There wouldn't be a dry eye in the plant!

"Well, anyway, as I said before, we manufacture specialty papers. We buy large rolls of raw paper, treat them with special coatings, and cut them into smaller rolls or sheets of pressure-sensitive stock. You probably see our product in the form of things like stick-on name tags, mailing labels, and postage stamps. Our plant runs three shifts five days a week, and we do about $110 million in annual sales.

"I thought a lot about what we learned here three months ago. After I realized what was involved, I had a

couple of concerns about going back and implementing this approach. We needed to reach critical mass
quickly. I thought if I practiced the three factors with
members of my senior management team, it would
eventually trickle down to people running the coaters
and slitters. On the other hand, I could get there much
faster if I had everybody on board right from the get-go.

"So I asked our friend Tony here to meet with
everyone in a leadership position — heads of account-
ing, sales managers, manufacturing team leaders, and
senior management. Tony was able to squeeze some extra
sessions into his schedule, so we split our people into
two equal groups and took care of things in a couple of
weeks' time. I have only sixty to seventy days' worth
of results to report, but those results are pretty good. In
fact, they're great.

"Our senior leaders and I decided that the two areas
that would bring the fastest improvement to the bottom line were manufacturing and sales. Coincidentally,
we had the most measures and readily available information in these areas.

"In manufacturing, we focused on two metrics:
productivity of the various pieces of equipment, and
scrap rate. When the manufacturing leadership team
met to discuss our approach, we realized we couldn't
just start putting up graphs and saying, 'We know we
can get this level of productivity and we can cut our scrap

rate to such-and-such a level,' then start reinforcing people and expect things to miraculously get better. So we worked with team leaders to create a short presentation on why the graphs were going up.

"After we finished our leader training sessions, we scheduled meetings with employees in smaller groups. Our most recent employee opinion survey told us that we weren't communicating with everybody as well as we should and that people didn't feel recognized for their efforts. So we started each meeting with a little rap on this theme. Kind of an ice-breaker. Then we went on to say that to improve communication and recognition we were going to put up some graphs that showed the productivity of each machine — many of which take two or three people to run — as well as product quality.

"We were already measuring both of these parameters daily. The shift superintendent was using the numbers for process control, but not for informational or motivational feedback. The operators saw only monthly summaries. And this situation screamed for the information to be displayed, because one of the things that directly affects these measures is teamwork and communication between shifts. So we told everybody we were going to put up graphs near each machine showing the amount of paper run per hour and the percent scrap, or waste. In the

> ❝
> **The shift superintendent was using the numbers for process control, but not for informational or motivational feedback.**
> ❯❯

end, we posted eight graphs at each machine — two for each shift showing productivity and scrap, and two 24-hour summary charts. That showed all of them how their individual teams did on each measure, and it showed them how they all did as one big team.

"We talked about how teamwork and communication between shifts affected everybody's performance, and how the graphs would enhance these factors. Team and shift leaders said they felt this would easily enable shifts to raise productivity by one-half percent and reduce scrap by one-half percent over the next three months. Then we asked the teams to aim even higher — to shoot for a full 1 percent improvement in both measures. We told them, 'You're skilled and experienced people, and you're already doing a good job. With these new communications in place and a little extra attention to detail, we are quite confident you can reach these goals.'

"We did this by meeting with manufacturing team members in small groups, six or seven people. The graphs didn't show targets at this stage, but as the discussions went on, the machine operators agreed that the goals were feasible, so they marked in the high-low target range. Further discussion revealed that they would prefer to measure this in negative terms — scrap rather than yield — because that's what they were used to."

Tony interrupted: "I normally recommend measuring positive units rather than negative, but in this case I felt it was better to go along with the operators' preference."

"Yes," said Carlos. "People were really beginning to communicate better, and we wanted to encourage that.

"So we used these meetings to build in all three factors. We created positive expectations, improved accountability with high-low goals, and established a positive feedback mechanism. Team leaders and shift superintendents are saying, 'I'm confident we can produce even better than we already are.'

"Now we've got accountability built into each machine — graphs for each shift's output, and graphs for daily output that account for teamwork between shifts. And our team and shift leaders take note of every improvement and reinforce it.

"Net result? Over the last sixty days, scrap is down three-quarters of a percent and productivity is up by half a percent. This translates to an additional $650,000 in profits annually. Teamwork is better. Motivation is higher. My own morale is higher.

"Now, we'd be very happy with this result alone. But we've also got sales. We have inside and outside sales, two people inside and nine outside. The sales manager established individual targets with each salesperson. We decided to measure sales volume, gross margin, and customer satisfaction. Overall sales volume affects overall revenues; gross margin percentage translates into profitability; and customer satisfaction measures whether we are truly meeting customer needs and not just pushing products at them. The sales manager set high-low goals in each area, which gave each sales rep three graphs of his own. Then in his office he had three companywide graphs showing all the sales reps' combined performance.

"In many ways, our sales results are even more impressive than manufacturing. Outside sales have risen by 1 percent. Inside sales? They're up 6 percent. But since outside sales come from a much larger base, this actually represents a larger revenue increase than inside sales. What's more, outside sales have a longer sales cycle, with larger accounts, larger orders, and a longer time before the extra effort pays off. So a 1 percent increase over sixty days probably means an eventual increase of 3 to 5 percent over what we would have gotten.

> **"**
>
> **Implementing and enhancing expectations, accountability, and feedback has added about $1.5 million to our bottom line.**
>
> **»**

"Our gross margin dollars are up by two-tenths of a percent. Together with the increase in sales, that means about $820,000 more in profit on an annualized basis.

"Which means that implementing and enhancing Tony's three factors — expectations, accountability, and feedback — has added about $1.5 million to our bottom line.

"Our intangibles are up, too. I've noticed that teamwork between departments is better, and communication has improved at all levels, both vertically and horizontally. The sort of thing you've experienced, Janet.

"You know, I had a feeling from the start, or at least after Tony began working with my execs, that people were going to like this. And a funny thing happened before we even got up to speed. As I said, we briefed the manufacturing teams and phased them in one at a time. Well, as soon as the first team got its graphs up, some of the other lines started asking, Hey, how about us? Why can't we have graphs that show everybody how we're doing?

"There really is this need to know. People want to be accountable. They want to know how they're doing, and when they find out, they want to do better. We think positive expectations make this desire even stronger. Accountability doesn't leave much wiggle room for laziness, but if you add positive reinforcement, nobody wants to be lazy.

> As far as I'm concerned, it's a million-dollar idea, and I've got the numbers to prove it.

"Now that we've made it part of our culture, Tony, I think this is great stuff. As far as I'm concerned, it's a million-dollar idea, and I've got the numbers to prove it."

# Mike's Classroom Story

## *Mentoring Kids for the Future*

"**M**ike, that leaves you," said Tony. "Is your assembly line pumping out more graduates now?"

Mike laughed. "Hey, I know you're joking, but these folks may not. I think too many schools are like Carlos's factories. No offense, Carlos, but kids are not rolls of paper. You can't just graph numbers of students and grade averages and graduations and SATs and say, hey, we're number one. You have to look at each student as an individual. You either fail or succeed, one student at a time.

"I love what I do — it's emotionally fulfilling, and I wouldn't trade it for anything. Although I must confess that it would sure be nice if there were more parents like Lloyd who let teachers know that their work is appreciated. And I guess I need to spend more time myself establishing parent-teacher partnerships, because it's the kids from those partnerships who are going to be the most successful.

"Anyway, to bring you up to date on my activities since the meeting. I've always believed we teach two things in school — academics and social skills. We teach knowledge and how to think about it, and we teach students how to get along in a civilized society. I think these are equally important. They aren't learned by accident; they have to be taught by design. And one supports the other. A kid who's doing great academically will not be happy if she doesn't socialize well. Ditto the kid who's popular but struggling with grades.

> "
> I've always believed we teach two things in school — academics and social skills.
> »

"So I wanted to test out Tony's three 'firstborn' factors in both areas. I wanted to see if high expectations, accountability, and positive feedback could make a significant difference academically, and I wanted to use them to help students become better adjusted socially.

"I chose my math class for my academic experiment because the grading is more objective than in other subjects. Although we give points for using the correct process, the math answers themselves are either right or wrong. Based solely on this academic measure, I would try to raise my class's scores by giving them lots of positive feedback whenever any of them improved his or her grade average.

"I started by telling the class I wanted to try an experiment for the marking period just beginning. I showed them a graph I had drawn of their average math test scores for the school year so far. The line jumped around a bit but the overall trend was neither up nor down. The overall average was 78.

"I asked them, 'What does this number mean? Does it mean that everyone in the class has averaged 78 on all tests?' After a few seconds one student raised her hand and said no, it meant that some could have averaged higher and some lower.

"'That's right,' I said. 'Just as some of us are taller than average and some are shorter, and some of us run faster than average and some slower. Now, the experiment that I want us to perform is to see if we can raise our combined average for this marking period to 81. That means some of you may be below that number and some above, but by working together we will bring the overall class average up to 81. Are you willing to try this experiment with me?' They said yes.

"Then they started asking all kinds of questions. What would happen if they averaged more than 81? 'Then we'll average more than 81,' I said. What if they averaged below 81? 'Then that's what will happen,' I said.

"They asked if I was going to post the scores. I told them no, just the class average. What would I do if somebody got a 60 on the math test? 'I'd mark a 60 on that person's math test,' I said. They got quiet and thought about it.

"When it became obvious they had no more questions and were curious to see what would happen, I suddenly decided to add one more element to the experiment. It occurred to me that I was outnumbered twenty-eight to one. For the experiment to succeed, we might need a lot more positive feedback. I asked, 'Would all of you be willing to make only positive comments about one another's math scores? For instance, if Pam got a 100, you'd say, "Great job, Pam," and if Scott got a 58, you'd say, "Don't worry, I know you'll bring it up next time." You'd never say anything to or about anybody that was a put-down. If you agree to this, I'll hold you responsible for it. What do you think? Are you willing to commit to this?' They all agreed.

"We were just getting into fractions, and we did some of our classwork in teams. I explained that the goal of the next lesson would be to convert fractions to percentages, percentages to decimals, and decimals back to fractions. And because I'm a believer in hands-on learning, I used things they could pick up and handle to learn. For instance, I provided box wrenches of various sizes, along with nuts and bolts. By experimenting with these, they could learn that $7/16$ inch was halfway between $3/8$ and $1/2$ inch. That's a much better — and more experiential — way to learn math than just writing numbers and lines on a chalkboard.

"For a typical team activity, I would provide a model or problem along with all the information they needed, explain the steps or principles involved, and guide them through a couple of practice runs. Then I'd turn them loose to work on it themselves. I'd hang around and watch closely enough to give them immediate and specific feedback — 'That's great, Doug!' or 'You're on the right track, Kate.' If I saw somebody wasn't getting it, or if someone was saying, 'I don't understand what I'm doing,' I'd say, 'Well, just show me your work and talk me through what you're doing so I can understand what you're thinking.'

"When students are working in teams, some are going to figure things out faster than others, or they may even know it already. I've found that these kids are often able to explain things to the others better than a teacher. I'm convinced that at least half of what kids learn in the classroom they pick up from each other. So sometimes, instead of helping them myself, I would turn to somebody else in the group and say, 'Dave, can you help over here?' or 'Who understands this well enough to show Carter how to do it?'

"With some of them learning and others tutoring, the kids really got their teeth into it. Yes, I know, you're probably saying to yourselves, he's just teaching teamwork. You're right. By adding that last part to the experiment, I ended up mixing academic and social learning. But that just goes back to my beliefs about the purpose of education. And I wanted as much positive reinforcement going on as possible — from everybody, not just me.

"Besides, they learned other things just as important as the academic and social skills. They learned that the real goal was not the test score — it was the understanding they were gaining, the skills they were mastering, on the way to getting the score. The score was just a marker along the way. There's a not-so-subtle difference, and once kids understand that, learning becomes much more interesting.

"How did my experiment turn out? Well, we didn't hit 81 — we blew right through it! Our class average was 83 by the end of the marking period. When I posted that on the bulletin board, with all the kids standing around looking up at it, they cheered — even though they knew about where we were going to end up because we'd been posting it all along! They were happy, their parents were happy — and I was happy. Plus, this time I heard good things from several of the parents.

> "How did my experiment turn out? Well, we didn't hit 81 — we blew right through it!

"One interesting thing. About halfway through the grading period, I invited all the parents to a meeting — more than half of them showed up, by the way, which pleased me — and I explained what we were doing and how preliminary results showed that positive expectations, accountability, and positive reinforcement were already making a difference. I told them I thought the same principles would work at home. Since that meeting, I've seen those students jump about two percentage

points in other subjects, so the parent-teacher partner-
ship thing seems to be taking hold.

"The other experiment I wanted to perform was
purely about social skills. I decided to work with one
boy who had a lot of trouble keeping his impatience in
check. Danny was a very competitive kid who would
get angry and aggressive when he didn't do as well as
others or live up to his own expectations. He would in-
terrupt, bang the furniture, and create disturbances.

"I had developed a trusting relationship with him,
so one day I said to him, 'You know, one of the things
I sense in you is that when you don't get things right the
first time or when you feel you're not winning, you get
really frustrated. And the reason I think that is because
I see you breaking your pencil, or shoving your desk back,
or talking loudly and saying some really inappropriate
and unkind things. Are you aware that this is going on?'

"He looked down at his desk and said, very qui-
etly, 'Yes.'

"I made it a point not to ask him why he did those
things. My goal was to get him to identify for himself
what he was thinking or feeling when he was acting that
way. If he could figure that out, I felt he could begin to
make some conscious changes and more appropriate
choices in his behavior.

"In my experience, kids are disruptive because they
feel insecure about themselves. It's a coping strategy, a smoke

screen. If they can get people focused on what they're doing, such as poking somebody with a pencil, then they can divert attention away from what they're feeling, which is more frightening. Perhaps they don't feel worthy or loved, or they're having a hard time learning and feel stupid because all the other kids seem to find it easy.

"I told Danny, 'I know that if we work together on this, you can control this behavior. Maybe you can replace it with another behavior that works better for you. Do you want me to help you try?'

"Again he said, 'Yes.'

"So I asked him, 'Do you get any kind of warning signals that this is happening? Like feeling more and more frustrated because you don't understand something? Or does it just happen all at once, without warning?'

"He said, 'Like, well, what are you talking about?'

"I said, 'Like your stomach might start hurting or feeling tight, or you might notice that you're clenching your teeth, or making a fist. These are signals. They mean you're starting to get anxious. And if you can see the signals, you can stop and say to yourself, "I need to look at what's going on here." And that will help you get in control of what you're feeling.'

"He wasn't sure, so I asked him to monitor himself over the next few days, and if he felt one of these blowups coming on, to pay attention to that. I told him I wasn't angry with him, but that I was concerned because he seemed to be feeling bad, and this would help him feel better. I said that seeing his behavior gave me a chance to sit down and talk with him about improving it and learning to handle it more successfully.

"Danny is a pretty savvy kid. He saw what I was talking about right away and soon learned to recognize the early warning signals. So we worked out a way to handle his frustrations. If it happened in the classroom, he would take four or five deep breaths. If he felt really tense, he would go get a drink of water, or — depending on what was going on in class — maybe just get up and move to the back of the room and work on something else for a while. If he felt he needed to leave the room, he would tug on his ear or maybe just ask to go to the restroom.

"And if I saw him getting tense without being aware of it, I would either look directly at him and tug on my ear as a signal that he needed to take a break, or if he was working in a group, I might come over and give him a couple of taps on the shoulder.

"**H**e was very competitive in sports and would lash out verbally or physically at anyone who got in his way on the playground. We talked about this and decided he should learn to back away from the situation, both mentally and physically. He would start by counting to three and backing up three steps. If he still felt tense, he would go to five, or seven, or ten. After that, he would stop counting and come see me.

"He said, 'It's kind of like a stop sign on the road, isn't it?' That gave me an idea. We took a digital camera out to the corner, and I took a picture of him in front of the stop sign, holding his hand up, signaling 'STOP!' We printed out several copies and laminated them on cards. He kept one in his pocket, another in his desk, and he took one home with him. Whenever he started feeling agitated, he would pull out a picture and look at it. Sometimes this was enough to stop the process in its tracks.

"Then I asked him to make up a little chart and to graph how many times he was getting tense each day. This piqued his curiosity, and soon he was becoming accountable for his own behavior and proudly giving himself feedback on how many times he was heading off trouble. Every day and every week that the number of incidents dropped, I praised his progress. If his behavior management chart showed that he had backslid, I told him I was glad he was keeping the chart accurately and honestly, and that I knew he would get back on track quickly.

> **Haphazard application of the three factors produces haphazard results, while systematic application produces substantial results.**

"In a few weeks, he went from five or six blow-ups a day down to one or two a week. Terrific progress. I consider this experiment a huge success. Truth is, it involves pretty much some of the same things I was doing before, but in a much more systematic way. So I guess one result of this experiment is something I learned: that haphazard application of the three factors produces haphazard results, while systematic application produces substantial results."

# Personal Commitment

## *Will You *Make a Difference?**

"Nice going, everyone," said Tony. "I'm very pleased by what you've accomplished, and you should be too. You've all done one of three things — succeeded with your project pretty much the way you intended, succeeded in a way you didn't intend —" he smiled at Lloyd — "or," nodding at Mary, "taken the appropriate action.

"This brings us to the end of the program. I've spilled all the beans I can spill, taught you everything I know. Except, of course, to answer your questions, comment on your observations, or hear your confessions. I always find these useful, and I always learn something new that I can pass along to the next group. Anybody have anything to share with the rest of us?"

"Actually," said Mike, "there's a little more to my story. I also teach piano, and I've started using these ideas in that area as well. I've always set goals for students to reach, but in the past they were single-target goals. Now my students and I are setting high-low goals together, and it's making a huge difference. For instance, I tell a student, 'Let's shoot for playing this passage three times in a row without missing a note. I know you can do it, because you've been practicing and I can see you're getting better. But let's also try to do one other thing, which is a little harder. Each time you play it, put a little more expression into it. More feeling. Once you've memorized the notes, start thinking about how you feel, how the music feels, each time you play it.'

"This works beautifully, for two reasons. First, it's a double goal — getting it technically correct, which is relatively easy, and playing with feeling and emotion, which leads to mastery but is more difficult. And second, it works because once they get it right, note for note, they stop being so anxious about that and start listening to what they're playing. In other words, their expectations go up, they become more self-confident, and they become open to interpreting the music and playing it artistically. This is very important — really, the most important thing — for a musician.

"I've also been thinking more about feedback. Piano is primarily an auditory medium, but teaching it also involves visual and kinesthetic prompting. Players need to position their hands a certain way in order to play with precision and strength. Students can learn this by feel, but sometimes it helps them to be able to see it. So I'm trying a new kind of developmental feedback.

"I simply videotape their hands for a few minutes. Then we watch the replay together. I reinforce them like mad when their hands are in the correct position, fingers poised over the keys, wrists straight instead of bent. This lets them connect how it looks with how it feels. For the few who don't pick up on this quickly, I say, 'Look how your hands are in the correct position here, here, here, and here. What's the best way for us to get your hands in that position all the time? I know you can do it, because I can see you doing it here. And you know you can do it, because you can see it, too. All we need to do is figure out how we can get you doing that all the time. What do you think? What's the best way to get there?' So I'm using both motivational and developmental feedback here, and the kids are learning faster. They're happier, too."

"Good examples, Mike," said Tony. "I'm going to put what you just told me in my teaching files. I get a fair number of music teachers in my class, and this will surely help them. Yes, Carlos? Go ahead."

"I have a story for the group and a question for Tony," said Carlos. "Tony mentioned earlier that I coach youth soccer. As you might imagine, my coaching style was a little heavy on accountability and light on the positive expectations and positive reinforcement. I won't go into details, but I was coaching more the way I had been coached as a youth and less the way that would best help my team develop. Then, after our first session here, I started paying more attention to positive expectations and positive reinforcement. Now, I can't say I never chew anyone out, but my style has changed considerably, and I've upped my positive-to-negative feedback ratio to four or five to one. A few of the players I once thought of as slow have really charged ahead. I also had a couple of kids who were pretty good but kept hogging the ball. I stopped yelling at them for that and instead started reinforcing them whenever they made a good pass.

> I was coaching more the way I had been coached as a youth and less the way that would best help my team develop.

"Our teamwork is a lot better now, and every player gets his teeth into the game. The players are learning more, enjoying the game more, and playing better, so we're winning more. At the kid level, winning is fun, but it's the other stuff that's really important — learning teamwork and the importance of practice and basic sports skills and ethics.

"Our company does community involvement things, so I decided to make our youth sports program our community involvement program for this year. We had Tony come in give a community talk. It was sponsored by the chamber of commerce, and we funded it. We invited business leaders, all the coaches — soccer, basketball, baseball, football, you name it — along with parents and educators.

"The response has been fantastic. We're now committed to bringing out the best in our community. Think about it: kids surrounded with teachers, parents, mentors, and coaches — everyone believing in the kids, holding them accountable for their actions, giving supportive feedback — working in organizations embracing the three keys that make everyone more productive.

"It's a huge task, and it's not easy. As Tony pointed out, the toughest part is changing our own behavior. On the other hand, the payoffs are sure worthwhile. The crossovers and links between family, schools, and business are really clear in my mind.

Carlos continued: "Anyway, that's my success story, and it's a pretty happy one. But in the company, I still have a few problem people. So here's my question for Tony: What do you do if you try all this stuff and somebody still doesn't perform? Do you fire them, like Mary did? And if you do, how does that fit in with the positive approach I see you advocating?"

"What we've been looking at here," replied Tony, "are ways of bringing out the best that people have to offer. But sometimes, despite everything you do, people don't offer you their best, or they're simply not able to do the job. Sometimes the best thing you can do for the person is give him the opportunity to succeed somewhere else. And the best thing for the organization, too. That decision is one you have to make dispassionately. Then you have to carry it out compassionately. Give the person the appropriate support to leave and find something somewhere else.

"The same thing applies for your community effort. There will always be youth coaches who think their task is to scream at every eight-year-old kid who's not doing things just right. There will always be a few parents who refuse to hold their children accountable for their actions. There will always be people who expect the worst, avoid accountability, and withhold supportive feedback. I don't have a magic wand to fix that segment of the population. So we just work with those who understand the right way to treat children, do our best to bring most of the others around, and keep the rest from doing more harm."

> **There will always be people who expect the worst, avoid accountability, and withhold supportive feedback.**

Mary said, "I find it really interesting that you coach soccer, Carlos. My husband coaches a Little League baseball team. After he helped me with our role play, he started thinking about his team and how these ideas might help, and he read my notes and asked me questions about this class. He admitted that he was probably a little hard on the kids — too critical, like you said. So he switched to just reinforcing what they were doing right, not just generally but very specifically — pointing out how one player was holding the bat correctly, how another followed through on his swing, how well the third baseman fielded that last ball. Instead of griping about how slowly they were learning, he told them they were becoming a good team. They've won three of their last four games, and more important, the kids are more motivated and having more fun. He's a true believer now — so, Tony, you'll see him here next month. He's decided he wants to learn it firsthand, and he's signed up."

"Great!" said Tony. "I like getting referrals, but two participants from one family is a real bonus. As long as there's no nepotism, of course." This brought a laugh.

Lloyd said, "Mary, you might be interested in my extracurricular experience. I got so juiced about how much better things were going with Lori that I decided to try something at the distribution company where I work. When a customer calls the inside order desk, we like our sales staff to suggest additional purchases, but they often forget, and the policy is only halfheartedly followed. I had a discussion with the three people assigned to that desk. We decided to post a graph showing the average number of line items per order, hour by hour and day by day — a lot like the charts you put up, Carlos. They took turns calculating it and posting the number. Every time it took an uptick, I reinforced the improvement. In the last three weeks, our average went from six items to eleven. Pretty good, huh?"

"Feedback in action," said Tony. "I won't even charge you double for using it at work, Lloyd."

Lloyd grinned. "I appreciate that."

"Well, I have a question and then an add-on bonus, too," said Janet. "First, the reason I'm here is that three colleagues of mine from a hospital over in Libertyville were here about six or seven months ago and suggested that I would enjoy the program. Shortly after our first session three months ago I e-mailed them to let them know how much I appreciated their recommendation. Then, just a few days ago, I talked to one of them, and she made a really interesting observation. Turnover in their three areas combined is down by 15 percent compared with the rest of the departments, and also compared with where they were six months ago. And yet none of them had turnover as a project. Any comments on that?"

Tony smiled. "Sure, it happens all the time. Had a company in here about a year ago — did maybe $700 million in sales, but turnover was costing them $12 million a year. Because turnover isn't on the profit-and-loss statement, it's often overlooked as an expense. But by the time you get through doing even a rough calculation

> **Because turnover isn't on the profit-and-loss statement, it's often overlooked as an expense.**

on training costs, time to get someone up to speed, productivity, and other costs, it can get pretty expensive. I'm not saying you want to eliminate turnover, because there's usually some people who should leave, and the occasional employee whose spouse gets a job offer that can't be refused. But most organizations have turnover that's higher than it needs to be.

"Anyway, we had most of their leadership team over several sessions, and the question of turnover came up. They were doing exit interviews, asking the 'Why are you leaving?' kinds of questions and getting the usual reasons for leaving — better pay, better job, and so forth. I suggested they ask a different question: 'When did you first think about leaving?' Then they started getting answers about not feeling appreciated and not being recognized for their contributions.

The bottom line is that, although they targeted other measures, using the three factors ended up cutting turnover 10 percent, which means that they dropped another $1.2 million to the bottom line.

"Very few people pick turnover as their project, but we do find that reduced turnover is a frequent outcome of putting the three factors to work.

"Whenever we've done a study or looked at the thousands of studies that have been conducted on what's important in your job, 'recognition for a job well done' is always near the top, and always ahead of 'money.' Think about it. Where would *you* rather work? At a place where they believed in you and your ability to succeed, where they outlined what they expected from you and then got out of your way and let you do it, where they let you know your efforts were appreciated? Or at a place with few or none of these attributes?"

"Whew!" said Janet. "Put it that way and it becomes really clear. Great. Now, then, my add-on bonus. I'm on a school committee, and lately I've been able to make a difference simply by using 'what' and 'how' questions. In the past, when people whined and said they didn't think we could do something, I would ask, 'Why not?' and they'd proceed to give me ten reasons why not, and we'd bicker until the meeting was over, and nothing ever got done. Last week, though, the idea of some joint teacher-parent projects came up. One committee member immediately said we shouldn't bother trying, 'because it's too hard to get parents to participate.' I simply replied, 'Yes, it's hard to get parents involved, but this project could really help, so what can we do to increase their participation?' Well, that changed the whole tone of the discussion. Instead of arguing about whether to undertake the project, we ended up talking about ways to increase parental interest and involvement in their children's education. Every time we hit a snag, I would come back with positive expectations and more 'what' or 'how' questions. I can honestly say that was one of the most productive meetings our committee ever had."

"A couple of things intrigue me." said Carlos, "First, I started out thinking that by taking this program I was going to be taking on more responsibilities at work. But this didn't really add a thing to my job. It's just a better way of doing it. Second, we all seem to be integrating this into other aspects of our lives."

"You're right on target, on both counts," said Tony. "The more you use expectations, accountability, and feedback, the more they become just the way you do things naturally. And if you think about their integration with other parts of your life, there's no surprise there, either. Before you know it, they become second nature to you. These three factors cut across all arenas.

> **This didn't really add a thing to my job. It's just a better way of doing it.**

"And the benefits multiply. Mike, take the twenty-eight kids in your class. Suppose that each year one of these kids decides to become a teacher and passes along the benefits to another twenty-eight kids a year over the next thirty years. Factor in the parents you'll affect, too. If you work that out, I don't know what you'll get, but it will be a very large number.

"The same goes for each of you. You now have the power to change many lives for the better, both directly and indirectly.

"Now, while you're reflecting on the enormous power in your grasp, here's your final exam. Surprised you, didn't I? Don't worry. There are only four questions, and you've got four minutes to think up as many answers as you can." He walked to the chalkboard at the back of the room and moved a chart, revealing four sentences he had written on the chalkboard:

1. Name the last three Heisman trophy winners.

2. Name any three Nobel laureates.

3. Name three people you've worked for or reported to who have mentored you in some memorable way.

4. Name three teachers who have profoundly affected your life.

Tony waited four minutes, then said, "Okay, pencils down.

"Now, I don't care about the names, but I want you to indicate how many names you thought of for each question. First question?"

Mike held up two fingers; Mary, Lloyd, and Carlos, one each; Janet, none. Tony turned to the chalkboard and scrawled the number "5" after the first question.

"Second question?" He counted the show of fingers. "Six? Is that all?" He wrote "6" on the board.

"All right. Third question. How many mentors stand out in your memory? Okay, great — three apiece. Yes, Janet and Carlos, I see that you're holding up six or seven fingers, but that doesn't count." Tony wrote "15" beside the third question.

"Okay, how many teachers? Seven, ten, eight, five, ten — Mike, don't take off your shoes, please." He turned and wrote "15" beside the fourth question.

"This is exactly the kind of response I get every time. Pretty revealing, isn't it?

"Each of the names you wrote down for questions three and four represents someone who made a difference in your life, someone who brought out the best in you. And over the last ninety days, each of you has made a difference for one or more people: the people you chose for your projects, and others you added on your own.

> **You have the power to make a difference in the lives of everyone you touch.**

"But this is only the beginning. You have the power to make a difference in the lives of everyone you touch. That's a choice that's open to you. I want you to choose to make a difference. And that's the real test, not the four questions you just answered.

"One year, two years, five years, or twenty years from now, when I guide five new people through this program, I want to see them write your names on this quiz."

# Free Download!

Want to start a dialogue with people in your school, company, or other organization? Feel like opening up a discussion with a colleague in another part of the country? Interested in talking about positive (or negative) expectations with your siblings? Has anyone asked you what books you've been reading lately?

Whatever the reason, if you want to help someone else understand the nature of the three factors, you can e-mail that person the first two chapters — free — by going to **bringing-out-the-best.com.** Then you can download the chapters for your own use or e-mail them to someone else.

# Notes and Comments

## Chapter 2

Here are several sources for more information on birth order:

If you're interested in the impact of birth order on major social change, creativity, and scientific advancement, read *Born to Rebel* by Frank J. Sulloway (Vintage Books, New York, 1997).

For more general information on birth order, consider *The New Birth Order Book* by Kevin Leman (Fleming H. Revel, Grand Rapids, Mich., 1998).

*Birth Order Blues,* by Meri Wallace, is written as a guide for parents to help their children adjust to different birth orders (Henry Holt and Company, New York, 1999).

The facts on firstborns come from a variety of sources. If you're interested in searching for more information, go to **psychinfo.com**, **webofscience.com**, or your local university's library system or media center.

## Chapter 3

Three classical sources of good information regarding positive expectations include the following:

*Pygmalion in the Classroom,* by Robert Rosenthal and Lenore Jacobson (Holt, Rinehart, and Winston, New York, 1968).

*Pygmalion Grows Up,* by Harris M. Cooper and Thomas L. Good (Longman, Inc., New York, 1983).

"Pygmalion in Management," by J. Sterling Livingston (*Harvard Business Review,* September 1988).

## Chapter 4

The MRE example and most of the GE information in this chapter were adapted from "Listen Up, Maggots! You WILL Deploy a More Humane and Effective Managerial Style," an article by Thomas A. Stewart in the July 2001 *eCompany*, which has since been absorbed into *Business 2.0*. The author is now editorial director of *Business 2.0*.

"Gradient stress" is a concept created by Professor Eugene Emerson Jennings of Michigan State University.

# Leader's Tool Kit

*How to Put the Lessons to Work*

This tool kit is designed to help you put the tools and techniques to work. If you just remember the three keys — believe in the other person, hold him accountable for his actions, and provide supportive feedback, you'll see a big difference in your impact on others and how they respond to you.

If you want to help others understand the nature of the three factors, you can e-mail them the first two chapters of this book — for free — by going to **bringing-out-the-best.com**. You can also download these pages for your own use.

## Educators, Parents, and Coaches

If you're an educator looking for ways to improve classroom performance, you can either think about the questions and answer them yourself or discuss them with other educators in a group. Parents and teachers can use the PTA/PTO as a vehicle for opening discussion groups, or even as a combined learning/fundraising project. Coaches can contact the National Alliance for Youth Sports in West Palm Beach, Florida, for additional support materials on coaching: **www.nays.org**, or phone 561-684-1141.

## Improving Company Performance

If you are in an organization, you can use the book as part of a "lunch and learn" program in which small groups examine how to perform better as a team. You can also use the book as an adjunct to a longer training program. See below for discussion guidelines.

# Guidelines for Conducting a Discussion Group

## *Preparing for the Discussion*

Discussions work best in small groups of five to eight individuals. If you're working with a larger audience, ask people to meet in small groups, discuss and record their ideas, then reconvene to share conclusions. A circular seating arrangement promotes interaction.

Prepare a list of the discussion questions. Write two or three questions on a flip chart for display during the discussion. Use questions from the list or generate your own. Print in large letters. The purpose of displaying the questions is to keep the group on track, much the way you would use a meeting agenda.

Share the questions with participants before the discussion. This will give them time for refection and allow them to refer to particular sections of the book. You may invite them to add other questions to the list.

## *Leading the Discussion*

Post the questions in full view of all the participants.

Pose one question at a time. After the conversation gets moving, try to take a back seat. Give the group control of the discussion. Avoid repeating the question unless the group gets off track — then refer back to the posted question. If people seem to be holding back, bring them into the discussion with a question: "Peg, what do you think about this?" Record all ideas suggested.

Summarize. Before you proceed to the next question, briefly summarize the main points you have discussed. Refer to the points that you captured in writing.

## Discussion Questions

The following are examples of the kinds of questions that help keep the discussion moving along. It's not an all-inclusive list, and the questions will need to be adapted to your particular situation.

### First Factor: Positive Expectations

In what ways do you *knowingly* communicate positive or negative expectations? Consider tone of voice, the actual words used, the setting, and nonverbal communications.

In what ways do you *unknowingly* communicate positive or negative expectations?

What positive or negative expectations do departments or functions have for each other? How can these be amplified or reduced?

If you could do one thing, starting today, to generate more positive expectations for someone else, what would that be?

Have you considered the possibility that your expectations for someone else, though not negative, are lower than what that person is truly capable of?

### Second Factor: Accountability

Let's start with a core issue. Do you hold yourself accountable? Are you as good as your word? If you can't answer, "Absolutely!" then start by holding yourself accountable for commitments you make.

Are the goals you set with others too high? Too low?

Are you using the high-low goal approach to encourage motivation and commitment?

Is someone accountable for the action steps that will ensure goal accomplishment?

Are you practicing the support principles associated with the concept of gradient stress?

### Third Factor: Feedback

Is your reinforcement timely?

Do you reinforce improvements? Oh, come on, now! Do you do it as often as you should?

Are you specific in your reinforcement?

Do you start with continuous reinforcement, then move to intermittment reinforcement?

Is your informational feedback goal-related, timely, and graphically represented?

Do you follow the five steps to "supportively confront nonperformance"?

Do you ask "what" or "how" questions that are oriented toward the future?

# About Tom Connellan

When companies like Marriott, Dell, and GE want to take their performance to another level, they all turn to one man — Tom Connellan. And with good reason. He's solid. Every year, he keynotes scores of meetings.

A former faculty member at the Michigan Business School and a guest lecturer on leadership at the Air Force Academy, Tom brings depth and breadth to your conference. As a company founder and former CEO, he knows firsthand what it takes to grow a business. Tom started a service company in the health care field and built it into a network of 1,200 instructors serving 300 hospitals and most of the Fortune 500 firms. He's worked in manufacturing and sales. Tom knows what it's like to be on the firing line of business, because he's been there.

Tom is the best-selling author of eight books and numerous articles. He's been the editorial director of four management and personnel magazines, a first-level supervisor, and a company president. Tom brings solid content and a passionate delivery style to his presentations. He captures the audience's attention and holds it from start to finish.

His proven techniques for pulling another 10 to 20 percent of performance have worked in company after company. Everyone leaves Tom's sessions with practical how-tos they can put to work the next day.

For information on schedule and availability, write to 2232 South Main, PMB 476, Ann Arbor, MI 48103; call 734-428-1580; or visit **tomconnellan.com**.

# Acknowledgments

This is the page where I get to thank those who contributed to this book. Where to begin?

Gary Procter, Pat Antonopoulos, Cindy Connellan, Elyse Kemmerer, Rob Weil, Pam Dodd, Toni Crabtree, Avis Fliszar, Miriam Bass, Cynthia Robbins, Pat Warner, Brian Harris, Richard Galiette, Nancy Bell, Gary Beckner, Fred Engh, and Bobbie Jo Sims all contributed to or read an early draft of the manuscript. The most brutal feedback came from my business partners Ron Zemke and Chip Bell, who enthusiastically — and lovingly — ripped it to shreds and provided ample suggestions on how to put it back together again.

Jenn Gaspari, Paula Noack, Carl Nickeson, Dawn Lipori, and Kathy Ferante all put heartfelt energy into the book. My program manager, Karen Revill, kept my office running smoothly and let me focus on the task of finishing the book. Peppy Dodd helped with her insightful observations at all stages of the manuscript. Helmi and Smokey endured my long periods of inattention and eagerly welcomed me upon my return to the outside world. Special thanks goes to friend and colleague Herb Cohen, who first introduced me to the performance characteristics of firstborns.

The editing, design, and production team of Ray Bard and Gary Hespenheide were great to work with. Special thanks to my editor and text designer, Jeff Morris, who continually found words in me that I didn't know were there.

And finally, a very special thanks to my loving wife, Pam Dodd, who not only gave valuable feedback at each step of the process, but also tolerated the intense focus required to finish the writing of this book — including the alarm going off at 5:30 on the "writing mornings."